TRANSPLANTED AND ARTIFICIAL BODY ORGANS

TRANSPLANTED AND ARTIFICIAL BODY ORGANS

Arnold Madison

BEAUFORT BOOKS, INC.
New York / *Toronto*

Library of Congress Cataloging in Publication Data

Madison, Arnold.
  Transplanted and artificial body organs.

  Bibliography: p.
  Includes index.
  1. Artificial organs. 2. Transplantation of organs, tissues, etc. 3. Reim-
plantation (Surgery) I. Title. [DNLM: 1. Transplantation. 2. Artificial
organs. 3. Implants, Artificial. WO 660 M182t]
RD130.M33 1981   617'.95   81-3805
ISBN 0-8253-0050-9   AACR2

Published in the United States by Beaufort Books, Inc., New York. Published
simultaneously in Canada by Nelson, Foster and Scott Ltd.

Printed in the U.S.A.   First Edition
10 9 8 7 6 5 4 3 2 1

Acknowledgments

The author would like to thank the numerous people and organizations who helped by providing information and other materials for this book. A special thank-you goes to *Dr. Robert L. Bernstein*, who from the inception of the project provided guidance on organization and opened avenues of research that would otherwise have been closed to the author.

CONTENTS

INTRODUCTION

In spite of almost daily news barrages about "medical miracles," few ordinary people really understand the full breadth of the medical discoveries and new surgical techniques that have been developed in the last twenty years. True, we have not yet reached a point where we can prolong life indefinitely, buying new body parts to replace worn-out, diseased, or injured organs, but that feat is not as farfetched as it may sound.

This book will touch upon three areas of medical science as well as their ramifications: transplants, implants, and replants. Transplanted organs are those which have been removed from one human being and placed into another person or taken from another part of the patient's own body. Implanted organs come from outside the recipient's body, but they are made from artificial material or a combination of synthetic substances and natural cells and tissue. Replantation, the most recent accomplishment of medical science, is a technique by which accidentally severed arms, legs, or fingers are restored. Not only is the body part replanted, but, in most cases, it regains some degree of normal function.

Several topics that might seem related to these subjects have been omitted purposely. For example, unless the disease or injury that weakened the organ is directly connected to its replacement, that disease or injury will not be discussed. Nor will the chapters touch on cosmetic surgery such as face lifts, which is quite a different discipline. The scientific achievements we are examining are so immense in scope that no one book could cover these subjects plus side issues, too.

Before we investigate today, let's take a look backward and learn how we reached this remarkable point in surgical history.

TRANSPLANTED AND ARTIFICIAL BODY ORGANS

One

THROUGH THE AGES

The dream of transplanting body parts to replace diseased organs or create new and more efficient humans is as old as the human race. In medical circles, there are those who joke about Adam and Eve, calling Adam the original *donor* and Eve the first *recipient* because she received Adam's rib.

Even while the Bible was being written, transplants were being carried out in India. The surgeon Sushruta, who lived one thousand years before the birth of Christ, wrote about his techniques in *Sushruta Samhita*. At that time, because of physical combat, diseases such as syphilis, or punishment for a crime, many people had lost their noses. Sushruta developed a skin transplant to replace that nose, a technique which would be remarkably like a technique discovered almost 2,500 years later and thought to be new. The Indian surgeon would take a plant leaf the size of the missing body part, place it on the patient's cheek, and trace around it with a marker. He then cut out the marked piece of cheek skin, leaving one end attached so that the piece formed a flap. At times, he would make a matching incision on the opposite cheek. Then, having "freshened" the stump of the nose with his scalpel, the physician folded the cheek tissue over the place where the nose had been and sewed the edges to the remains of the original nose. Two thin tubes were inserted into the new nose to act as air passages and to provide shape to the skin. The transplanted tissue and sewn edges were treated with powder of sappanwood—an East Indian tree—barberry, and licorice root. Covered with cotton, the nose was left to regenerate. As soon as the cheek skin was united with the other facial tissue and healed, the flap was detached from the cheek.

Sushruta does not mention how he developed the skin-grafting technique or if experiments had been attempted to graft skin from one person to another. In some way, however, he happened upon the perfect transplant. As will be explained in Chapter Two, our bodies "accept" transplants from portions of our own anatomy, but may "reject" transplants from other people or animals. Also, the skin flap would continue to be nourished by the bloodstream while healing because one end had been left attached to the face.

The ancient Greek people, who gave the world the Father of Medicine, Hippocrates, achieved some spectacular medical feats, too. They developed what may be called an artificial bladder. The bladder collects urine from the kidneys and discharges the fluid from our bodies. If the urine builds up within the body or is unable to travel from the kidneys through the ureters to the bladder, our system may be poisoned by the unreleased waste chemicals. Both the ancient Greeks and Romans used catheters, small tubes that can be inserted through the urine tract. Archaeological specimens of ancient catheters have been unearthed in Ephesus, Asia Minor, and Pompeii, Italy. The ancient instruments were constructed from bronze, copper, and silver. Later pewter, wood, and processed leather would be employed. Even though most ancient cultures from the Chinese and Hindu to the Babylonians realized that urine tests could be a diagnostic technique, it was the ancient Greeks who developed the means of collecting a urine sample before it was excreted from the body as well as an artificial bladder to replace an inoperative bladder.

The device is still used today, although in a slightly different method. Flexible catheters were developed in the 1700's by the surgeon general to Frederick the Great, who made them from rubber (one of the earliest uses of this New World substance). Today, the ancient Greek device can be the means of testing the urine from each kidney separately to determine if both kidneys are operating with equal efficiency.

With the fall of the Roman Empire in A.D. 476, Europe and the field of medicine fell into the Dark Ages. Scientific progress halted, and instead of dreaming about transplanted organs, the few learned people who survived hoped only to maintain the knowledge they already possessed. Most cures, passed along through the ranks of ordinary people, were based on superstition. Moss from a dead criminal's skull was a highly prized medicine for many ailments. "Weapon salve" was a concoction rubbed on the blade that had caused the wound rather than on the wound itself. Legends from the Middle Ages tell how a master who had lost a nose in battle could grow a new one by forcing a slave to donate his. However, there was one serious drawback. The slave owner had to keep the donor alive and well because, if the noseless slave died, so did the transplanted nose, shriveling and dropping from the master's face.

Possibly there is some historical basis to these tales. Some masters may indeed have tried to transplant noses from slaves, and when the mutilated slaves died and subsequently the transplants did not take—rejected by the recipients' bodies—the results were fancifully interpreted.

With the coming of the Renaissance, medicine experienced a rebirth. Unfortunately, there had been a regression in certain skills and techniques, so some "new" discoveries were actually rediscoveries of centuries-old concepts. But, once started, these advances in medicine and surgery were pushed forward steadily by such famous medical schools as that at the University of Salerno, Italy—a movement that would eventually carry medicine into the 1980's.

In the sixteenth century, an Italian surgeon, Gasparo Tagliacozzi, developed a technique for transplanting skin to the nose. (The apparent obsession throughout ancient times and the Middle Ages with noses stems from the fact they were often lopped off in battle or in duels, and also because it may have been the only transplant that succeeded. Scientific literature of that period does not carry reports of other experiments, but they may have been attempted and then abandoned when they failed.) His method was much like the technique utilized by the ancient Indian surgeon, Sushruta, except that, instead of a skin flap from the cheek, the tissue was cut from the upper arm and set in place. This made life a bit difficult for the patient, because he had to keep the arm in an upper position with the hand resting on the skull until the transplanted tissue healed. Then when the transplanted skin flap received blood from facial vessels, the grafted skin was disconnected from the arm.

4

Tagliacozzi's discoveries and the work of other scientists made skin transplants—even those executed between two different people—quite common by the 1800's. Meanwhile, medicine continued advancing. Until successful surgery was a reality, transplants on a major scale would only remain a dream. Each new discovery improving surgical technique, although not planned as such, carried science a step closer to artificial and transplanted organs. In the sixteenth century, Ambroise Paré's development of ligation enabled surgeons to control bleeding. This knowledge added to that of William Harvey's determination of the circulatory system in 1628 was a giant step forward. Ether was first used as an anesthetic in the 1840's, and Joseph Lister's introduction of aseptic surgery in 1867 meant many more patients were now surviving operations.

If surgery was moving steadily forward, so was the dream of scientists to transplant portions of the body to replace diseased or injured parts. In 1869, Jacques Reverdin was a young Swiss intern at the Hospital Necker in Paris. While treating patients with ulcers, Reverdin observed that, unexpectedly, new "islands" of skin would begin growing in isolated spots of raw wounds. He wondered if it would then be possible to speed recovery by transplanting bits of healthy skin to the ulcerous areas. A patient was admitted with an injured thumb that had a small wound over which no new skin would grow.

Reverdin cut two pieces of skin—each a millimeter square—from the patient's arm and planted them on the thumb wound. The skin sections were held in place by a strip of lead plaster. Recovery was swift and amazing. Within a few days, the transplanted skin had grown to the edges of the wound. A week later, the new skin had sealed its edges with the old thumb tissue. Elated with his success, Jacques Reverdin named his surgical process *greffe épidermique* or skin graft.

5

Scientists around the world were thrilled with the concept of skin grafts, and for the next thirty years grafts were made from the patients' own bodies or from animals. But when doctors saw skin grafts being rejected by certain patients, while other people healed successfully, the graft process lost favor. Few people attached any importance to the fact that the skin grafts where the skin was brought from the same body were the successful ones. Autografts, as these were named, were almost always the means of having a patient recover quickly. But why?

An important clue was to come in 1882, when the Russian scientist, Elie Metchnikoff, was vacationing on the shores of the Mediterranean near the Strait of Messina. One day while his family went to a circus to see some famous performing apes, Metchnikoff worked in his laboratory. A casual observation on his part was the first step in solving the great puzzle of why transplanted organs so often did not "take."

Metchnikoff was studying the mobile cells of a transparent starfish larva when he suddenly found himself wondering if there might be cells present which protect the organism against foreign invaders. He introduced a splinter into the larva's body. Returning to his lab the following morning, he peered through a microscope and saw cells attacking the germs on the splinter. What he had discovered were the white blood cells, which function as defenders of the body. Such defenders are vital to preserving life, of course, but they are the basis of the rejection syndrome that creates failures in many transplant operations. Elie Metchnikoff was to receive the 1908 Nobel Prize in Medicine for his research in immunology.

If scientists had not yet discovered organ transplants, fiction authors had. Dr. Victor Frankenstein, hero of Mary Shelley's 1818 Gothic novel, actually built a human being out of parts stolen from corpses. The novel's viewpoint reflects the strong religious opposition to using parts of one human body in another person. There is a story that hundreds of years ago, a soldier had a section of his skull replaced by bone from a dog's skull. Shortly after the operation, a heavy deluge struck the area, and the man was almost hit by lightning. The church officials interpreted the near-miss as divine anger against such medical feats, and they ordered that the bone be immediately taken from the man's head. Whether this story is apocryphal or not is unimportant. Its pertinence lies in the fact that the Church (hence nearly everybody) believed there was something intrinsically evil in body replacements.

Literature reflected this attitude. In the early 1900's, when the first shrunken heads of the Jivaro tribes were brought from the Amazon Basin to Europe, they caught the public fancy, and shrunken heads began to be featured in magazine fiction, always possessors of evil power. The trend continued in science fiction of the early and middle twentieth century—stories where scientists transplanted the brains of humans into the skulls of apes to give them super intelligence. Another favorite fantasy theme is that of the human being rejuvenated by acquiring transplanted monkey glands.

Fiction and science combined to form a new type of transplant, which may be the ultimate in medicine—transplanting a whole body. For decades, scientists have known that lowering the body temperature slows down the rate at which the body organs work. What if the body was lowered to a temperature where the organs "slept"? A person with a fatal illness such as cancer could be preserved until such a time as a cure had been found for his disease. Cryogenics was born—at least in science fiction. Stories began to appear in magazines about people who were frozen and then awakened years later after their children and friends had died.

During the 1960's and 1970's, when medical achievements such as heart transplants and artificial body parts became a reality, a subtle shift occurred in fiction. Transplants and artificial body parts were presented as beneficial and desirable. An entire TV series, *The Six Million Dollar Man*, was based on the concept of a shattered body recreated with mechanical parts. Steve Austin, its bionic hero, used his superpowerful body to fight evil.

Why the change in attitudes?

Probably because science fiction had become science fact.

For centuries, doctors were able to replace certain body parts with artificial organs that worked. Glass lenses corrected some forms of faulty vision, and false teeth enabled their owner to chew hard foods. If a person lost an arm or leg, mechanical limbs could be attached. At first, these had no mobility and were often mere tools—a peg to replace a lost leg, a hook for a hand. But slowly artificial hands or legs were developed that could operate in limited ways. However, scientists still held the dream of transplanting body organs.

A French surgeon took the first step toward making it a reality. Dr. Alexis Carrel had been trained as a doctor, but he was more interested in research than in treating patients. In 1902, he devised a way to sew cut blood vessels end to end, so that they carried blood as efficiently as they had before an operation. This is a major step in any organ transplant today. For this discovery, he received the Nobel Prize for Medicine in 1912. In 1913, Carrel successfully transplanted a kidney from one cat to another, the first scientific attempt at organ transplant. Later, working with Charles Lindbergh, he developed the perfusion pump, a device for keeping donated organs alive until they could be placed in a recipient. Without these two advances—joining of blood vessels and perfusion pump—transplant operations would be impossible.

With the discovery of the human blood groups in 1901, for which Austrian pathologist Karl Landsteiner received the 1930 Nobel Prize in Medicine, and the subsequent knowledge of the Rh factor in blood gained in the 1940's, blood transfusions became one of the most successful transplants. Few writers mention blood transfusion when exploring the subject of transplanted organs, perhaps because the procedure is taken for granted today. But blood transfusions are indeed true transplants in themselves. And not only that. They also make many other transplants possible.

These advances in medicine, as well as the technological production of synthetic materials, moved medical science to the brink of the Age of Transplanted and Artificial Body Organs.

Two

TRANSPLANTS

Today, the surgical profession has the know-how to remove practically any organ cleanly from a donor's body and transplant that organ into a recipient. The time when people can have new kidneys, hearts, livers at need is just ahead.

Regrettably, we have been on the edge of this medical miracle for some years now. Why can't we move that single last step forward?

Because we are literally our own worst enemies. The human body's very capability of fighting off infection and disease causes it to reject the transplanted organ.

For hundreds of years, people have known that victims of certain diseases, once recovered, would never again develop that disease. The Turks were the first to take advantage of this concept by inoculating healthy people with vesicle material from a smallpox victim, thus inducing a mild case of the disease and conferring permanent immunity. In 1718, the practice was introduced into England by the wife of the ambassador to Constantinople, and during the eighteenth century it gained some limited acceptance in Europe. But it was not until 1798, when Edward Jenner demonstrated that the same effect could be produced by the relatively mild cowpox virus, that the idea of inoculation to prevent various diseases gained popular consent.

That significant advance is based on the ability of our lymphocytes, or one of two types of white blood cells, to remember they had once attacked a particular invader in the blood system. Unfortunately, they also recognize new invaders.

During the late 1940's and early 1950's, doctors discovered how to transplant kidneys. The bright, initial success dimmed as the bodies of most patients rejected the new organs. In 1953, Drs. Peter Medawar in London and F. Macfarlane Burnet in Australia made a discovery for which they won a joint Nobel Prize in 1960: the immune mechanism. Every cell of a substance—whether it is a virus or pollen or human tissue—carries what may be called chemical flags. These flags or *antigens* are what alert our lymphocytes that something alien has entered our system. For example, a virus enters our body and carries different antigens than those found in our tissues. Our lymphocytes then attack the invader. But the lymphoctyes recognize the antigens that are present in our cells and do not attack those cells. These antigens are known as the "human leukocyte locus A" or HLA antigen. There are four distinct types: HLA-A, HLA-B, HLA-C, and HLA-D. And these four categories break down into many smaller ones. For example, one person might have HLA-B27 while another individual could have HLA-B8 in his cells. These antigens vary greatly from person to person so that they become a biological fingerprint.

The antigens work for our benefit in transplants from one portion of our body to another, such as skin grafts. Our lymphocytes recognize the familiar antigens and do not attack the transplanted skin. But if the skin from another person, who may have different antigens from those of the recipient, is placed on the body, the lymphocytes detect the foreign bodies and attack the transplanted skin. The transplant is then rejected.

What can be done to overcome the rejection syndrome?

Not as much as doctors would like or enough to insure totally successful transplants. That is the wall preventing us from entering the Age of Organ Transplants.

First, since antigens are genetically produced, they are determined by heredity. Therefore, identical twins have matching sets of HLA antigens, and organs can be transplanted from one twin into the other without the tissues being identified by antigens as foreign. That is known as an *isograft*. Among other siblings, including fraternal (nonidentical) twins, the chances for a perfect HLA match is about one in four. For unrelated people the odds are a thousand to one that an isograft can be made.

The HLA compatibility of donor and recipient is tested when organ transplants are contemplated, but the tests are not infallible. They seem most reliable in predicting success when the two individuals are related.

If the rejection syndrome arises, doctors may attempt to suppress that reaction in any of several ways. One method is to administer cytotoxins. This word translates as "cell poisoners," and it is appropriate because cytotoxins retard the work of the lymphocytes. This is a dangerous technique, however, for beneficial as it is to the transplantation process, it also weakens the individual's ability to fight other infections. The patient may then fall victim to such illnesses as pneumonia or the very disease that destroyed the original organ.

Another class of drugs, corticosteroids, can be given to the patient. These are a mixture of natural and synthetic substances that resemble cortisol (hydrocortisone), a hormone produced by the adrenal glands. It does not attack the lymphocytes but works against the inflammation that results when the lymphocytes attack a foreign organ. Again, however, this undermines the patient's ability to resist infection.

One of the most recent techniques is *extracorporeal* (outside the body) *irradiation of the blood*. Scientists have known for years that X-rays kill lymphocytes. In fact, X-rays were the first means used to combat the rejection syndrome. However, there was no way to destroy the lymphocytes without injuring other parts of the patient's body. Now a tube is placed in the patient's brachial artery (in the arm), and the blood is allowed to flow through a tube where X-rays destroy the lymphocytes. The treated blood then flows back into a vein further down the patient's arm. Fewer rejections occur in patients who have extracorporeal irradiation of the blood before receiving a transplant operation. But, as with all the other techniques, there is no guarantee of complete success.

The solution to the problem of rejection syndrome still eludes researchers, but their work continues. Some studies have been done with progesterone, a hormone produced in a woman's body chiefly during ovulation and pregnancy. Pregnancy is the big exception to the rejection syndrome. Theoretically, a fetus should be rejected by a woman's body, because half of it is composed of foreign proteins. Scientists are not sure why it is not. Does a woman's body produce a special substance to prevent the rejection? If so, is it the progesterone hormone? Infusion of progesterone in

14

the site of the transplant has, in some cases, halted a rejection.

Other scientists wonder if it's possible to treat the donor's organ in some way to reduce its antigenic strength, so that it does not trigger a rejection. Until now most attempts to prevent or halt rejection have centered on the recipient's lymphocytes. Experiments—some successful, others unsuccessful—involve treating the donor with massive doses of cytotoxins before the organ is removed. This is called *preneutralizing* the organ.

Research also continues in perfecting our method of matching up donor and recipient antigen-wise. In October 1980, three scientists were awarded the Nobel Prize for Medicine for their experiments in identifying antigens. Drs. Baruj Benacerraf and George D. Snell as well as Dr. Jean Dausset of France received the honors because their research will not only advance medical science toward successful organ transplantation but on a larger scale in prevention of many diseases which may be antigen-linked.

However, until a foolproof means is devised to prevent rejection, the Age of Organ Transplants must remain just a dream.

BONE GRAFTS AND BONE MARROW TRANSPLANTS

Many people view bones as dry and dead, a mere framework to support flesh. But bone is living tissue, its cells undergoing an unending cycle of being destroyed and replaced.

Bones are classified in two ways: degree of hardness and shape. *Compact* bone is extremely hard while *cancellous* bone is spongy. *Flat* bones are like those found in the head. They are composed of two layers of compact bone enclosing a center of cancellous bone. *Long* bones like those found in our legs have a hard, tubular exterior with an internal cavity filled with marrow.

As with any living tissue, bones require nourishment. Tiny blood vessels penetrate the periosteum or tough, fibrous membrane that envelopes the bone, and they continue deeper, weaving through the bone to the marrow. Only plasma, rather than whole blood, bathes the bones' cells, and plasma contains only fluid without suspended particles (red and white blood cells and platelets). As a result, with a bone transplant, there is no need to match donor and recipient, because no danger of the rejection syndrome exists.

In 1890, a Scottish surgeon, Dr. W. Macewen, made the first successful bone graft or transplant. Three years before, he had removed a diseased section of a youngster's upper arm bone. The missing portion did not regenerate, and the boy's parents asked Dr. Macewen to amputate the useless limb. Rather than do that, the doctor transplanted pieces of spongy bone that he had removed from other patients, rebuilding the missing portion of the arm bone. The doctor was thus able to save the limb. Ironically, when the boy grew into adulthood, he earned his income by doing heavy manual labor.

Today, severe fractures are sometimes rebuilt with pieces of compact bone or a dentist can rebuild portions of a patient's jawbone. With some people, pieces of spongy bone can be cut from pelvic bone, but most often surgeons make use of bone banks, which can provide either dead bone or live bone. To maintain cell life in a bone, the bone is stored at a temperature from 0 degrees to −250 degrees. For years a debate raged about whether or not this kind of live bone—or the patient's own transplanted bone—lived on in the recipient's body. Researchers finally determined that, no matter what type of bone is transplanted, the transplant dies. Therefore, bone transplants are mere building blocks to fill gaps in a natural bone or to prevent the growth of scar tissue, which would hinder the bone's regenerative ability to grow new bone cells.

The red marrow of certain bones in our bodies is virtually a factory, manufacturing millions of red blood cells and platelets per minute. The red cells are needed to carry oxygen to the body cells, while the platelets enable the blood to clot. Several blood diseases are caused by infection attacking the marrow or by malfunctioning bone marrow. The best-known and most devastating of these is leukemia, which shuts off normal marrow operation. Both red cells and platelets are decreased in a leukemia victim's body, as the lymphocytes (one type of white blood cell) increase. As a result, the person dies of anemia (lack of red blood cells) or of severe bleeding.

Sickle-cell anemia is a hereditary defect in the formation of normal red blood cells. Each year, approximately 80,000 children around the world die from the illness. The disease occurs mostly among African tribes and blacks in the United States, but some Caucasians have been known to be inflicted. Sufferers rarely live beyond the age of forty. The name stems from the fact that the red blood cells, which contain an abnormal hemoglobin molecule, have an odd crescent shape, resembling a sickle blade. Other scientists refer to these diseased cells as "oat-shaped." As the mal-formed cells pass through the blood vessels, they hook onto the vessels' inner lining. Eventually, the number of cling-ing cells builds up, cutting off the blood flow to an organ. Victims of sickle-cell anemia usually die from the failure of a vital organ such as the kidney.

Still a third blood disease occurs in a child who is born with a weakness in his immune system. Formerly, such youngsters were destined to die in infancy, because there was no means to protect them from infection. Now they, like victims of leukemia and sickle-cell anemia, are being helped by transplanted bone marrow.

Dr. Georges Mathe, a French doctor, was the first to experiment in treating leukemia with transplanted bone marrow. In the early 1960's, Mathe began to treat several patients with severe cases of leukemia, warning them that his treatment was highly experimental. He first gave them heavy doses of X-rays to kill the leukemic cells. Next, he transplanted the marrow. Although all these first patients were to die eventually, the transplant did alleviate the disease for a short period. And, by 1968, doctors in all nations were beginning to understand the value of this procedure and had begun to transplant bone marrow.

Today, there are approximately twenty cancer centers in the United States that treat leukemia with bone-marrow transplants. One of the most successful is the Fred Hutchinson Cancer Research Center, which is connected with the University of Washington School of Medicine. In September 1980, Dr. E. Donnall Thomas, the head of cancer therapy at the University of Washington School of Medicine, addressed an international symposium on cancer that was held in New York City. Dr. Thomas described his typical patient as a cancer victim who has had a relapse after chemotherapy treatment. Once this occurs, the prognosis generally is poor without a bone-marrow transplant. The method of treatment is similar to that introduced by Dr. Georges Mathe. The doctors administer massive doses of anticancer drugs and radiation to the leukemia victim. Healthy bone marrow is infused into the patient after two or three weeks. If it "takes," the marrow will start forming new blood cells.

Bone-marrow transplanting has helped many patients with sickle-cell anemia and leukemia, but perhaps its greatest success has been with children born without a strong immunal system, thanks to Dr. Robert A. Good, now president and director of the Sloan-Kettering Institute for Cancer Research in New York City. Although one type of white blood cell, the lymphocyte, is manufactured in the lymph nodes, spleen and the intestinal tract, another family, the granulocytes, are produced by the red marrow. The granulocyte might be compared to an amoeba. When bacteria invades the body, this type of white blood cell moves through the capillary walls by shrinking, expanding and tugging themselves. Once they encounter the bacteria, the granulocytes engulf and digest the invader. Dr. Good's pioneering in the field of bone-marrow transplants which provides a means for the body to produce the granulocyte cells, has been the means of saving the lives of thousands of children who would have died from an infection their bodies could not fight.

A bone-marrow transplant has strong positives but also one serious negative aspect. The positives include the fact that transplanting bone marrow is one of the simplest of the transplant operations to execute. No drastic surgery is needed, no expensive efforts to store the donated marrow. All the donors are alive, and as the bone marrow is withdrawn from the breastbone and hipbone, the material is pumped into the recipient through a tube into the abdomen, where it is absorbed by the lining of the abdominal cavity. The negative aspect is the problem of matching, which is more essential in a bone-marrow transplant than in most others.

However, the facts that live donors are used and that both the recipient and donor are known far ahead of the operation help overcome the negative aspect. There is time for thorough testing so that the two people are as closely matched as possible.

CORNEA TRANSPLANTS

One of the most successful stories in the world of transplanted organs is that of corneal transplant—where the cornea (or "window" of the eye) is transplanted from a dead donor to a living victim, whose own cornea has become injured or diseased. The cornea is the transparent portion of the eye that covers the pupil and iris and admits light. Certain infections or accidents, such as chemical burns, can cause a cornea to turn cloudy or be destroyed. To a victim, it is as if he were peering through a frosted shower door, seeing only vague shapes. Worldwide, corneal disease is the most common cause of blindness, children being the most frequent victims. Fortunately, even youngsters can receive corneal transplants. Successful operations have been performed on infants as young as five months old.

Why are almost all corneal transplants—today numbering in the tens of thousands—so successful?

Because there is practically no danger of the recipient's body rejecting the donor's cornea.

The cornea has no connections with the blood supply. Its nourishment is derived from the eye fluid. In fact, in those cases where a disease has caused blood to surround or enter the cornea, even a corneal transplant will not restore sight. The presence of blood continues to obscure the vision.

Surprisingly, the first successful transplant occurred on an animal. In 1835, a British army surgeon, S. L. Bigger, was being held prisoner by a group of Arabs when a pet antelope became blind because of a scarred cornea. Another animal of the same species was brought in wounded but not yet dead. When the second antelope died, Dr. Bigger removed its cornea and transplanted it into the pet antelope. The operation was a success, and ten days later, the animal indicated clearly that it could see.

Corneal transplants in humans can be made from fresh cadavers, as Dr. Bigger did with the antelope. In the majority of transplants, however, the donor has died days or weeks before the recipient is ready to receive the transplant. If the corneal tissue is to be used within three or four days, it is preserved at 4 degrees Celsius. If a period of weeks must pass, it is stored at −196 degrees Celsius, the temperature of liquid nitrogen, until it is needed.

The problem of bringing the cornea down to −196 degrees without doing damage was at first knotty. As the temperature drops, portions freeze while other parts still remain as tiny pockets of liquid. The chemicals there are extremely concentrated and may be either highly acid or highly alkaline. As a result, there may be chemical reactions, harming portions of the soon-to-be transplanted cornea. All the tissue's fluids have to be kept liquid for as long as possible. In other words, an "antifreeze" is needed.

Research produced that antifreeze—dimethylsulfoxide (DMSO)—and today it is used for corneal tissue as well as other types of tissue awaiting transplantation. DMSO is not strong enough to preserve a whole organ, however, even a whole eye. The cornea is cooled to 4 degrees Celsius, placed in a 12 to 13 percent DMSO freezing medium, which is also maintained at 4 degrees Celsius. The temperature is then dropped quickly at the rate of 1 degree to 10 degrees per minutes until it reaches −60 degrees Celsius. Now the DMSO has frozen, and the cornea can be transferred to a liquid nitrogen refrigerator, where the temperature is −196 degrees Celsius. Later, when the tissue is rewarmed and transplanted, the results will be identical to that of using a cornea from a fresh cadaver.

Corneal transplants can alleviate another health problem, also. Victims suffering from extreme cataracts often must have the natural lens of the eye removed. Vision until now has been restored with thick cataract glasses, recently developed contact lenses, or plastic lenses implanted inside the eye. Today, medical science offers still another alternative. A new technique called keratoplasty, can restore vision by implanting "spectacles" in the eye itself.

Keratoplasty was developed by Dr. José Barraquer of Bogota, Colombia. Dr. Barraquer has operated successfully and apparently with permanent results on victims with severe near- or far-sightedness and with patients whose lenses have been removed because of cataracts. In the United States, the procedure is still considered experimental, especially to cataract victims. However, as word of successful operations spreads, surgeons who employ this technique expect that more and varied use will be made of keratoplasty.

The operation consists of removing a bit of the patient's cornea, inserting another slice of the donor's cornea, which has been shaped into a lens, and then replacing the tiny piece of cornea that was removed. The surgeon has literally put a living lens into the patient's eye.

One hospital in the United States that has developed a highly successful keratoplasty program is Holy Cross Hospital in Mission Hills, California, under the direction of Dr. Richard A. Villasenor. In June 1980, Dr. Villasenor described the operation by saying, "It's like putting a pat of butter between two pancakes." The pancakes are two clear layers of the patient's own cornea, and the butter is the donated slice of cornea "lens," which is placed between them.

As can be imagined, the operation is extremely delicate and is carried out by means of a microscope. A wire brace holds the patient's eye open. First, the surgeon uses a tiny brush to mark a reference line on the eye's surface. Then, a metal ring is fitted over the eyeball. The ring holds a track for the blade of an electronic knife called a microkeratome. Slowly, skillfully, the surgeon slices the precisely measured bit of cornea. Using the reference mark, the doctor then realigns the bit of cornea and sews it loosely into place with a curved needle held by tweezers.

Before the operation began, the surgeon had removed a tiny sliver of the donor's cornea. Placing it in a $50,000 Barraquer cryolathe, the doctor then "grinds" the frozen corneal slice so that it can function as a lens for the eye. Now that piece—dyed bright green for visibility purposes—is slipped under the sewn corneal piece, and the threads are tightened. The last step is to sew the eyelid shut. This will be for only a few days and is a precaution so the patient doesn't squeeze the eyelid or rub the eye, dislodging the lens. The full results are not known until about six months later, but so far the $3,500 operation has helped many persons both in the United States and South America to regain their sight.

The story of corneal transplants is indeed a success story. But the bandage-removing scene we see so often in motion pictures, where the patient immediately shouts, "I can see again!" is seldom so dramatic in real life. The return of sight comes in stages over weeks and months. But in at least 96 percent of the cases, vision does return.

Thus from its early beginnings in the nineteenth century to conventional corneal replacements to complicated operations like keratoplasty, this medical procedure has enabled many people, who would have been partially or completely blind, to live full lives once again.

HEART TRANSPLANTS

Ironically, the type of transplant which first excited the world about the possibility of organ transplants is today one of the most seldom undertaken. In spite of an enthusiastic launching of heart transplants, many heart specialists now frown on this operation.

Heart transplants had an early, if abortive, start. In 1905, the French scientist, Dr. Alexis Carrel, removed the heart of a small dog and attached it to the neck of a larger dog. The donated organ continued to beat for several hours. Carrel did no further experiments on heart transplants, although he did manage to keep animal heart tissue alive in a test tube for thirty-eight years. Then almost thirty years after that first experiment, researchers at the Mayo Clinic continued Carrel's work with dogs. Here, too, the attachment site was the neck, and again these hearts functioned successfully for a few hours. But there seemed little possibility of replacing the original heart by implanting the new one at the same site.

In 1961, Dr. Norman E. Shumway of the Stanford University Medical Center, California, moved science a large step ahead by being the first person to place the hearts actually into the bodies of the recipient dogs. The operations were a success, and the animals survived—until the rejection syndrome arose. The importance of Dr. Shumway's achievement is not only that for the first time a heart was implanted into a donor's body, but that he developed a method of attaching the donated heart that is still used in human heart transplants.

In order to understand heart transplants, it is important to remember the heart's structure. There are four chambers of the heart. The upper two are the right and left atria (formerly called auricles), and the lower two are the right and left ventricles. Blood flows *into* the atria and *out* the ventricles—into the left atrium from the lungs and out by the left ventricle (via the aorta) to the entire body; into the right atrium from the body and out the right ventrical (via the pulmonary artery) to the lungs, a perpetual circulation.

The heart transplant patient is connected to a heart-lung machine, which carries the blood from the right atrium to a chamber where the carbon dioxide is removed and oxygen added to the blood, normally the duty of the human lungs. The blood then returns to the patient's body and continues its usual flow. The machine thus takes up the functions of both the heart and lungs of circulating and purifying the bloodstream.

Now that the recipient's heart is being bypassed, surgeons can remove the heart by cutting the upper part of the right and left atria. The donor's heart is taken out in exactly the same way and is attached to the remaining part of the right atrium. The left atrium is next connected and then the two arteries leading from the ventricles of the heart, the aorta and the pulmonary. The clamps, which had been in place to prevent the patient's blood from entering the heart, are removed, the machine is detached, and normal blood flow is restored. An electrical charge is applied to make the heart begin beating at a normal rate.

In 1964, Dr. James Hardy of the University of Mississippi performed a heart transplant on a human being for the first time. He removed the heart from a ninety-six-pound chimpanzee and placed it into the body of a sixty-year-old man who weighed 180 pounds. Although the operation was successful, the transplanted heart beat for only an hour because the organ was too small to accommodate the amount of blood in the man's body.

However, even though most people were unaware of the fact, scientists knew that a human-to-human heart transplant was not only the next step but imminent. Dr. Norman Shumway and his associates at the Stanford University Medical Center were fast approaching this next step, but they wanted to undertake more research before risking an actual transplant.

The stage was set for the drama: Scene: Groote Schuur Hospital, Cape Town, South Africa. Time: December 3, 1967. The actors: the relatively unknown Dr. Christiaan Barnard and totally unknown Louis Washkansky. Dr. Barnard transplanted the heart of a man who had recently died into Mr. Washkansky's body.

Washkansky died eighteen days later. But Dr. Barnard's

second patient, Dr. Philip Blaiberg, a dentist, lived for nineteen months after his December 1967 operation.

Not only was the ordinary person electrified by Dr. Barnard's stunning success, but many heart specialists viewed the technique as the wave of the future. Within a year of Christiaan Barnard's two initial operations, one hundred heart transplants were performed around the world. But then in the next few years, the numbers dropped off, almost by half each year. Some surgeons refused to undertake such an operation, treating patients with more conventional techniques and sending them elsewhere if they insisted on the transplant operation.

Why?

First, there has alway been the problem of finding donors. Each year approximately 600,000 people in the United States die from a coronary heart attack. Many of these lives might have been prolonged if donor hearts were available. But the donor heart has to be in excellent condition, and the donor's immune system must match that of the recipient, and this combination is hard to find. Persons who might wish to contribute their organ after death may be too old or diseased to qualify or they may die at a time or in a place with no patient awaiting the transplant. Sometimes relatives intervene. The donor may have made only an informal statement, not a written and signed declaration, about his wish to donate an organ. After the individual dies, the family rejects the request and follows normal funeral arrangements.

But in addition to donor difficulties, the results of heart transplants were disappointing in terms of longevity. Few transplant patients live for more than two years after the operation. Admittedly, such individuals are thankful for two additional years, but a number of heart specialists do not feel the success rate warrants the cost and risk of a heart transplant. Rejection accounts for many deaths, while other transplant patients, taking heavy doses of antirejection drugs, die from infection. Another frequent cause of death is coronary artery disease, to which long-term transplant recipients seem especially susceptible.

There are still flurries of interest in heart transplants. In the spring of 1980, British surgeons scored a rousing success by transplanting organs into seven heart patients (an eighth patient did not survive the operation). Both the English people and those in medical circles demonstrated renewed enthusiasm over heart transplants. But how will they view the process in two years or five years?

At the present time, the answer to heart replacement seems to be an artificial heart. However, if the rejection syndrome can be overcome, perhaps once again heart transplants will be more widely employed.

KIDNEY TRANSPLANTS

Each day our kidneys unobtrusively go about their job of cleansing approximately 190–200 quarts of fluid without attracting the attention that we pay to other organs such as the heart. Yet these two bean-shaped organs, weighing approximately half a pound each, are instrumental in preventing the body from poisoning itself with an accumulation of its own harmful end products.

Most people are familiar with the shape and deep-maroon color of kidneys, having seen veal or beef kidneys at meat counters. Human kidneys, measuring about five inches in length, are located behind the abdominal cavity and are protected by the lower ribs and a cushion of fatty tissue. Each kidney is composed of a million microscopic filters, nephrons, which create an exquisite filtration plant. Fifteen times a day our entire internal environment passes through the kidneys, where the nephrons separate out waste materials such as excess salt, ammonia, urea, and uric acid. The entire 200 quarts of fluid, except one quart, is then returned into the bloodstream. The quart containing the waste products and harmful chemicals becomes urine and flows through two small tubes called ureters into the bladder, where it is held until excreted)

If one of the two kidneys becomes damaged and unable to function, the other can continue working alone without seriously disabling the body. Unfortunately many kidney disorders affect both organs.

What happens if both kidneys cease to function normally?

When kidney failure occurs, urea and salt begin to accumulate in the blood. Too much urea causes nausea, vomiting, and weakness, and excess salt creates swelling in the face and legs. Inoperative kidneys also raise the potassium level in the bloodstream, and overabundant potassium can eventually stop the heart. Death from kidney failure is most painful and prolonged. Approximately 10,000 Americans suffer incurable kidney failure annually, and these people would be virtually sentenced to death if no way had been developed to replace the diseased kidneys.

Over a period of years, beginning in the Netherlands during World War II, the artificial kidney was developed, a device which filters waste from the bloodstream of persons with nonfunctioning kidneys. The artificial kidney saves lives, but dependence on it is difficult, expensive, and time consuming, costing hundreds of dollars a week and several hours per session.

Then, in 1954, the first kidney transplant took place. Ronald Herrick donated a kidney to his twin brother, Richard. The operation was performed at the Peter Bent Brigham Hospital, Boston, and recently the three surgeons who executed the successful transplant, Drs. J. Hartwell Harrison, John P. Merrill, and Joseph E. Murray, were

28

On the twenty-fifth anniversary of the first successful kidney transplant, the original team of doctors was honored. Left to right: Dr. J. Hartwell Harrison, Dr. John P. Merrill, Dr. Joseph E. Murray, Dr. George Thorn, Dr. Francis D. Moore, Dr. Gustave J. Dammin.

BRIGHAM AND WOMEN'S HOSPITAL

honored at the twenty-fifth anniversary of the first successful kidney transplant. The Herrick operation worked out fine because transplants between identical twins are almost always successful. Ronald Herrick lived a normal life with only one kidney, and his brother Richard survived with the transplanted organ. Since then some 25,000 kidney transplants have been performed in the United States!

Kidneys are one of the easiest organs to transplant. Un-

29

like other transplanted organs, the malfunctioning kidney does not have to be removed. The transplant can be placed in any body cavity, such as at the base of the throat, although the usual placement is in the right pelvis. The blood supply to the kidney is simple, consisting of one or two arteries and one or two veins for each organ. And there is only a single outlet to be attached—the ureter.

Unfortunately, the supply of donated kidneys is inadequate for the numbers of patients who could benefit from such transplants. As public awareness grows, the supply rises, but it still cannot meet the demand. Yet the reason to expect more donated kidneys is strong. First, kidneys can be obtained from people in good health rather than from cadavers, and when a member of the family has experienced kidney failure, there is strong motivation for close relatives to volunteer. Secondly, guaranteed success for organ transplants between family members moved much closer through a discovery made at the University of California, San Francisco (UCSF), in April 1980.

In an attempt to fight the rejection syndrome, doctors at the research center conducted experiments on thirty patients who were to receive kidney transplants from family members. Within a six-week period prior to surgery, the patients each were given three blood transfusions from the donors, in hopes of desensitizing their immune systems. These thirty patients were watched carefully over a two-year period, following their transplants, and it was found that only one patient had died. And the dead person had also been a diabetic and had stopped taking essential medication following surgery.

"This was a revolutionary approach," said Dr. Oscar Salvatierra, chief of the Transplant Service of UCSF. "It had not been tried in humans before because the opposite result was feared—that the [transplanted] kidney would be rejected immediately."

Officials at UCSF refused to speculate on the exact numbers of patients who will now qualify for kidney transplants because of the success of this new procedure, but they expect a proportionately great increase.

How is a kidney transplant performed?

If the donor is living, the organ is removed in one operating room and rushed to an adjoining room where the transplantation takes place immediately. But when the organ is taken from a dead donor, a more complicated process is needed.

The donated organ can be kept "alive" for about three days at the most. (If the organ comes from a person who experienced a sudden death, doctors can still revive the kidney almost one hour after the death.) The kidney is first cooled to 10 degrees Celsius. Lowering the temperature further than that would lengthen the period the organ could be preserved, but there would be a harmful side effect. The water within the cells freezes at 5 degrees Celsius, causing the cells to expand and explode. Tissue damage would make the organ useless for transplantation.

The removed kidney then goes through the perfusion process, in which a nutrient fluid is pumped through it. Whole blood—the blood given in transfusions—would seem to be the logical perfusion fluid, since it is the one employed by the living body, but natural blood thickens at the cool temperatures and the red blood cells burst. Thus whole blood works for only a few hours. Plasma, the clear, slightly yellowish fluid in which the cells are suspended, works best in perfusion, carrying nutrients throughout the organ. A drug is added to the plasma to protect the kidney from infection, and dextrose is present to supply energy to the cells. To assist the organ in the utilization of the sugar, insulin is also added to the perfusate.

The perfusion machine used to pump the nutrient through a donated organ can be the standard floor model,

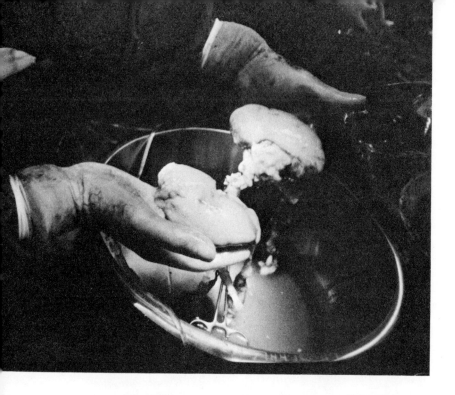

Packed in plastic bags and surrounded with ice, kidneys remain "alive" for at least twenty-four hours, and up to three days.

about the size of a Xerox copier. But Dr. Folkert O. Belzer of the University of California has invented a portable perfusion apparatus that can keep a kidney alive up to seventy-two hours, and for transporting kidneys, Dr. Lawrence Stevens of St. Luke's Hospital Center, New York, developed a transport box. The kidney (or other organ such as a liver) is placed in a half-gallon jar filled with iced saline solution. The jar is covered with two plastic bags and then ice is packed all around the jar. The outer covering can be a polystyrene cooler like the inexpensive type used by people to keep sodas cool on picnics.

The perfused donor kidney is now ready to be placed in

the recipient's body. As mentioned earlier, the most common resting place for the new kidney is the right pelvis. The surgeon makes an incision just below the navel, extending the line to the end point just above the right hipbone. The blood supply for the new kidney will come from a vein and artery in the leg. The last step is attaching the ureter so the urine can drain into the bladder. And then both the patient and the doctor must wait to see if the transplant will "take." The next weeks, months, and years are filled with tests to determine whether the recipient's body is going to accept the transplanted organ and if the organ will function effectively.

Although kidney transplantations are one of the more successful of organ transplants, the results are not perfect. Organs donated by family members have about an 85 percent success record after two years. The lowest rate is for those people who received a kidney from a cadaver. Here the number is about 60 percent. Many patients who have undergone a kidney transplant continue to require machines to keep their blood cleansed of harmful materials. At the present, artificial kidneys still maintain a higher success potential than the transplanted kidneys.

LIVER TRANSPLANTS

The liver is the largest solid organ of the human body, weighing about four pounds and occupying the upper part of the abdomen beneath the diaphragm. The organ is divided by a fissure that creates a small, tapered left lobe and a much larger right lobe. The liver is comparable to a chemical factory, possessing the ability to modify almost any chemical substance. However, breaking down toxic molecules in our bloodstream is only one function of the liver. The organ is a blood reservoir as well as a storage plant for vitamins and digested carbohydrate or glycogen.

This is released to maintain blood-sugar levels. Our liver manufactures enzymes, cholesterol, proteins, Vitamin A, and blood coagulation elements. And, in some cases, it is able to undertake red-blood-cell production. Perhaps its best-known function is the production of bile, an orange-yellow fluid that has a bitter taste. Bile plays an important role in digestion by emulsifying fatty materials so they can be absorbed by the intestines.

Diseases of the liver include jaundice, which is an excess of bile in the circulatory system, and cirrhosis, where the scarred liver tissue cannot handle the salt in the body's system. In some cases, a liver may develop a benign or malignant tumor, which interrupts its vital functions of detoxifying poisonous materials and storing iron. Unfortunately, an artificial liver is not yet available, so for certain patients, a transplanted liver is the only hope.

The world's first liver transplant was accomplished in 1963 by Dr. Thomas Starzl, who is still the leading surgeon in that field today, conducting approximately twenty-five transplants each year at the University of Colorado Health Sciences Center, Denver. A recent case at CU is typical of many liver transplants undertaken at the school's medical center.

In May 1980, twenty-year-old Cheryl D. desperately needed a replacement organ or she would die from a four-year bout with an illness that traps blood inside the liver, thus enlarging the organ. A phone call came from Seattle, Washington. An eighteen-year-old accident victim, who had died in an automobile collision, was available to donate a liver. Both the donor and the recipient had type O blood, so the possibility that Cheryl's body would accept the transplant was good. The parents of the dead victim had agreed to a request from the Northwest Kidney Center to donate the victim's liver. Time was crucial, however. Although officially declared dead, the donor was still in the hospital's intensive-care unit, connected to the life-support systems that kept his heart beating and the liver "alive." Once the organ was removed from the body, the liver had to be transplanted within ten hours. Since the victim's body could not be detached from the life-support machines, and Cheryl's condition would not allow her to leave the hospital, a team had to be sent to retrieve the donated liver.

Removing and packaging a donor's liver is a delicate medical process, requiring people thoroughly trained. The team in this case consisted of four members: an intern; a resident assistant; Paul Taylor, the coordinator of the transplant program; and Dr. Starzl himself. Dr. Starzl tries always to accompany transport teams of this kind, so that he can personally oversee the retrieval of the donated organ.

With the exactness of a military campaign, plans were made—timing plane arrivals, arranging for cars to transport Dr. Starzl and his team, and making preparations in both hospitals for operations on donor and recipient. Both Colorado and Washington law-enforcement officials cooperated, as did airline and airport workers and even weather forecasters, and with their help a split-second schedule was worked out.

The four men rushed to Denver's Stapleton International Airport to take a night flight to Sea-Tac (Seattle-Tacoma) Airport. Arriving in Seattle, the Denver team was rushed to a car. Each person carried plastic cases containing instruments and materials necessary to the retrieval. One man held a plastic container which still displayed its original label: "Double Six-Pack Cooler." This was the case that would transport the liver to Colorado. The team drove along Interstate 5 to the Providence Hospital in Everett, Washington, where the victim's body lay.

The countdown to ten hours began the moment the donor's four most important veins and arteries were cut. The removed liver was then carefully inserted in the plastic container, which held an iced saline solution. This in turn was packed in ice to maintain the cold temperature and thus keep the liver alive during the return journey.

Now the four-man team retraced its tracks, speeding back down Interstate 5 to Sea-Tac, a 7 A.M. return flight to Denver, then a six-hour operation to place the donated organ in the body of ailing Cheryl D.

Later, Dr. Thomas Starzl learned that he had racked up forty-six hours from the beginning until the end of this mission. But thanks goes not only to Starzl, who has been described "as one of the best—if not the best—pair of hands in the country," but to Paul Taylor, who coordinated the entire retrieval process, and the many concerned individuals who did their bit to expedite the retrieval trip. Cheryl's operation succeeded nicely.

Although such rigorous trips are a normal part of Dr. Starzl's professional life, there is nothing routine about a liver-transplant operation. In fact, except for the lung, the liver may be the most difficult of all transplants—exceeding the intricacies of a heart transplant, because the liver's blood vessels are much smaller than those in the heart, and therefore, more difficult to sew after being severed.

Many surgeons insist that someone past the age of forty-five cannot have a successful liver transplant, nor can the donor be beyond that age. Success rates for Dr. Thomas Starzl's program are about 55 to 65 percent for children who are fifteen years old or younger. For adults, the numbers slip a bit to around 40 to 50 percent. Nevertheless, because of the problem of finding donated livers for youngsters, approximately 70 percent of the transplants conducted at the CU medical facility are on adults.

What is the future for liver transplants?

The major problem, as indicated above, is finding donated organs. Today, only organs from cadavers are used, because a donor would die without a liver. But in some experiments, partial liver transplants have been attempted with dogs, cats, and monkeys. Since the liver has remarkable regenerative powers, as much as one-half of the donor liver can be removed and still allow the donor to survive. If these partial transplants prove feasible, then the use of live donors will be possible in certain cases. The timing of such operations would also be much simpler than the urgent missions that Dr. Thomas Starzl's team must now undergo. But until that time, liver transplants will have to be conducted with organs from deceased donors by means of a frantic race against the clock.

LUNG TRANSPLANTS

Fifty-seven-year-old Harold W. was a patient in the Albany Medical Center, New York, and he was dying. The cause was emphysema, a disease that strangles the victim—the feeling has often been compared by sufferers to drowning. The walls of the air sacs in Harold's lungs had stretched and become flabby, with "blebs" (bubbles or blisters) forming. As a result there was a decrease in his ability to absorb oxygen and eliminate carbon dioxide. With every exhaled breath, Harold's lips pursed—a trait common to emphysema victims—because pursing the lips helps remove more air. Placing Harold on a heart-lung machine would help briefly, but there is no way for his lung tissue to regenerate, so connecting the patient to a mechanical device can only forestall death for a matter of days.

Prognosis?

Death.

The only alternative would be a lung transplant. Unfortunately, lung transplants are the most difficult to undertake of all transplant operations, and, as a result, the success rates are also the lowest.

Our two lungs lie on either side of the chest cavity. In

appearance, they are cone-shaped, grayish in color—unless the person lives in an urban area or is a heavy smoker, in which case the lung tissue becomes black. Their bases rest on the dome-shaped diaphragm, and the tops are in the root of the neck. The functioning part of the lungs is the air sac. There, the carbon dioxide is removed from the blood, to be expelled by the exhaled breath, and oxygen is added to the bloodstream flowing back into the heart. This exchange requires only 1/1000 of a second. The walls of the air sacs are the area where this exchange takes place. If spread out, these sac walls in a single human being would cover a space of eighty-four square yards.

In addition to emphysema, often caused by cigarette smoking, cancer and silicosis can also attack the lungs. The latter is a chronic disease of people who work in areas where there are large amounts of quartz or coal-dust particles. Also, being around asbestos can lead to asbestosis. Both silicosis and asbestosis have the same effect. The lung tissues become hard and brittle and are unable to absorb oxygen. Victims literally suffocate.

In 1906, Alexis Carrel, mentioned earlier in relation to the first heart transplant in an animal, also conducted the first lung transplant in a dog. The first lung transplant in a human was accomplished by Dr. James Hardy in 1963. Working at the University of Mississippi, Dr. Hardy removed a lung and transplanted it into a recipient, who lived eighteen days. That time period may seem very short, but not when discussing lung transplants.

Why is there such a discouraging lack of success?

Numerous reasons. First, the storage of a donated lung is more difficult than storage of other organs. A kidney, as we have seen, can be stored and perfused before transplantation to a recipient. But if a lung undergoes perfusion, the cavities soon fill with water. Cooling it, as other organs are refrigerated, does not help significantly. Therefore, it can only be a matter of hours from the time the lung is removed from the donor until it is implanted in the recipient. Although donors can live with one lung, few people are willing to sacrifice one while they're alive.

Because there is so little time between the removal and transplantation, the matching of the donor and the recipient is often impossible. As a result, a high number of transplanted lungs are rejected by the recipient's body. When a transplanted lung begins to fail, other major organs such as the kidneys, liver, and heart are adversely affected by the oxygen loss, while the brain is destroyed by a build-up of carbon dioxide. Thus lung failure can produce multiple problems, any single one capable of killing the patient.

Harold W., mentioned at the beginning of this section, will be receiving a lung transplant. A donor from his own family has agreed to sacrifice one of his lungs, but both donor and recipient realize the odds against success. Yet they are odds the family is willing to face as must all recipients of a lung transplant until such time as further research has increased our ability to succeed in this difficult operation.

SKIN TRANSPLANTS

The liver is the largest *solid* organ of the human body, but the largest organ per se—consisting of approximately twenty square feet in an adult—is the skin. Many people never think of the skin as an organ. Yet the word "organ" is defined as a collection of cells that perform a particular set of functions, and the human skin certainly meets that definition. Not only does it serve as a wrapping, holding our internal environment together, but it protects us from infection, regulates the temperature of our bodies, and even acts as an "early warning system" by alerting trained eyes to the first clues of illness.

When comedian Richard Pryor suffered extensive burns over the upper half of his body in June 1980, newspaper and television newscasts kept public attention focused on the sophisticated surgical techniques used to save him.

Severe burns are one of the main causes of death for people under the age of forty and the third leading cause of death for all age groups. The grading of burns is done on the basis of first-, second-, and third-degree, with the seriousness intensifying as the level moves up the scale. A first-degree burn is about like a bad sunburn. The skin reddens and is painful, and ultimately peels, but there is no serious threat. Second-degree burns destroy the top layers of skin. They are more painful and serious, often leading to permanent scarring.* A third-degree burn is one in which all the layers of the skin are destroyed, and this is what Pryor suffered.

The victim of third-degree burns is immediately rushed to the tanking room of the nearest burn center, which is equipped with troughlike tubs. There the wounds are gently bathed and evaluated. Swelling can be a serious problem. If the tongue swells, the breathing tubes might become clogged, and a similar problem, often caused by smoke inhalation, might affect the vocal cords and larynx. If so, a tube is inserted down the throat for breathing or an incision is made to alleviate the condition.

During the first twenty-four hours, patients are often fed intravenously with a salt solution to combat serious dehydration. Infection is also a potential problem to severely burned people, since the burned areas are skinless and open to invading organisms. So burned areas are coated

*Immediate and proper treatment is needed. The American Red Cross, in its manual *Standard First Aid and Personal Safety*, recommends the burns be cleansed in cloths dipped in ice water and wrung out, and then a clean dressing should be applied. No ointments or sprays should be applied to a second-degree burn.

with newly developed drugs such as Sulfamylon, Silvadene Cream, and Betadine foam to destroy the bacteria.

Then the third-degree-burn patient is ready for the next step, which is grafting. First- and second-degree burns require no skin transplants, since new skin grows up from under layers to replace what has been destroyed. But in third-degree burns, these under layers, too, have been burned away, and thus a replacement of the natural skin is necessary.

There are several types of skin grafts. One has already been discussed—pedicle grafts, the kind that the ancient Indian surgeon Sushruta and the Renaissance doctor Tagliacozzi employed, in which one end of the transplanted skin is left attached to the original site. This is also called a full-thickness graft, because the full layer of skin is transplanted to the new location.

The thickness of human skin varies, depending upon the location. The thinnest skin is only 1/16 inch thick and is the type found on the eyelids. The thickest skin layer is 1/3 inch thick and is the kind which is located on the back of the neck. For a full-thickness graft, the doctor removes the entire layer of skin, baring the flesh underneath, while a split-thickness graft requires only that the epidermis or top layer of skin be transplanted.

The most succesful skin grafts are accomplished by using the patient's own skin, such as was done with Richard Pryor. Skin was removed from his calves and thighs, and this new skin was stretched over burned areas on his shoulders, chest, back, arms, and ears. In this type of grafting, entire sections are removed to cover the wound like a sheet. In other circumstances, small patches about an inch square are placed over the injury checkerboard fashion. These pieces eventually grow and unite into a solid layer of skin.

If the patient has too little surviving skin to supply his

own grafts, then doctors must obtain skin from a skin bank. There are now ten such banks in the United States. Live donors or cadavers supply skin to these banks. If a dead donor is used, the skin must be removed within twenty-four hours after death to insure that the tissue is still biologically alive. A thin layer of skin about four inches wide—almost identical in thickness to the skin that peels away after a sunburn—is taken in strips from the donor's body and legs by means of a device called 'a dermatone, an instrument with a razor-sharp blade. When rolled across the skin, the dermatone cuts any thickness of skin desired and rolls up the piece. The dermatone is so sensitive it can slice off as little as 15/1000 of an inch. With a cadaver donor, the only skin portions taken are those that have been kept covered after death.

The skin is then treated and slowly frozen to −189 degrees Farenheit, so that it can be preserved for up to a year. When needed, it is thawed and microscopically cut into pieces so that a small strip can be stretched across a wide area. In the healing process, the skin covering fills in, much like newly planted grass. As the patient is healing, his body may reject the donor's skin, but by that time it may be possible to make skin grafts from his own body.

Once the skin has been obtained for a graft, the victim has to be prepared for the transplant. First, the wounds must be cleansed of the charred flesh. Again surgeons employ the delicately honed dermatone, with a blade no more than 1/20,000 inch thick. During the removal of the useless skin, a great deal of blood is usually lost, which is why several skin grafts are usually required with individuals as badly burned as Pryor. At the present time, experiments are being conducted in cutting away the burned skin with several types of miniature lasers. There is much less blood loss with lasers than with the dermatone.

Even after the skin transplant has been accomplished, serious problems can arise. There is a constant danger of pneumonia and diseases that waste the body. Ironically, burn patients, who are maintained on an extremely nutritious diet, may suffer from malnutrition. The reason is that a burn injury requires tremendous number of calories to heal. Doctors used to urge burn victims to eat many steaks, milk shakes, or omelets, but the results were discouraging. Today, a nutritious fluid is pumped directly into the patient's stomach twenty-four hours a day until the danger of malnutrition is past.

As news reports of Pryor's treatment were published, readers were confused by the fact that the victim, in spite of being on the critical list, was nevertheless walking around and taking special baths. But it is essential in burn treatment to keep the patient moving during the recovery period, because if the healing skin is left immobile, it may grow too tight, preventing the patient from bending his arms, legs, or fingers. And it is one of the peculiarities—indeed, one of the horrors—of severe burning that the patient remains lucid through the worst of it.

For a burn victim suffers appalling pain during his recovery period. The movement of the skin and the ungrafted wounds is agonizing, the daily baths in the hydrotherapy tanks—necessary so the old dressings can be removed and replaced—are an excruciating experience. In fact, mere air moving over a burn injury can cause the victim torture.

In skin transplanting, there is an additional psychological problem for the victim. Ugly scarring is almost impossible to prevent, and as the patient moves about to keep the skin flexible, he may well pass a mirror. The sight of himself half-healed may badly shatter his nerve and cause him to need strong emotional reinforcement.

Doctors are working on the scarring problem. Special

pressure masks—including ones that cover the entire body—have been tested. These are designed to maintain a constant pressure on the wounds so that scars will not form. However, pressure masks are not always successful.

Plastic surgery, after the victim has recovered from the initial burn injuries, will clear away the scar tissue itself. But grafted skin contains no hair follicles, nerve endings or sweat glands. And even with much exercise during the recovery period, the elasticity of the transplanted skin is never as great as that of the original skin.

As we know, skin transplanting was the very first type of organ transplant to be developed and today remains one of the most widely used. Annually 300,000 Americans are hospitalized for severe burn injuries, and for some, skin grafting is their only hope for recovery.

SPERM BANKS AND REPRODUCTIVE ORGAN TRANSPLANTS

The use of sperm banks and artifical insemination is not usually viewed as a transplant, because it is not the recipient, the female, who has the faulty reproductive system, but her mate. However, sperm banks do provide the means whereby material from one body is implanted in another in order to overcome a physical bar to normal function. And, in 1977, medical history was made when a true reproductive-organ transplant was successfully completed.

Tim Twomey of Sacramento, California, was born without testicles. As he matured and married, he had to receive painful testosterone shots each week in order to maintain his masculine sex characteristics. However, even these shots were not sufficient to enable his body to produce sperm. In 1977, Twomey underwent an operation which removed a testicle from his identical twin brother and attached it to Tim's body and reproductive tract. The urologist who performed the surgery, Dr. Herbert Cronin, used a technique that was derived from experiments with rats and in vasectomy reversals. The operation had never been tried before, so the patient was warned not to become too hopeful about the outcome.

"When sperm was produced," Twomey said later, "everybody was amazed."

On March 25, 1980, thirty-three-year-old Twomey became a father when his six pound, fourteen ounce son, Christopher, was born.

In spite of the success of the Twomey case, Dr. Cronin doubts that there is much future for testicle transplants. "It was like making a bet of a million-to-one and winning," Cronin said later. The circumstances—involving an identical twin—were so unusual that doctors do not expect them to recur often enough to establish a pattern of treatment. Testicle transplant will not become common until the immunological problems leading to rejection have been solved.

Therefore, a couple who wish to have a child, and are unable to utilize the husband's sperm, must resort to artificial insemination. Tens of thousands of women have received sperm through this technique, and the husband's infertility has not always been the reason. The father may be known to have a genetic defect, which he does not want to pass along to his child. Or Rh factor may cause problems for a couple. An Rh negative woman married to an Rh positive man (especially if she has become sensitized by having a transfusion, abortion, or previous pregnancy) risks a miscarriage or the birth of an abnormal baby if she becomes pregnant by her husband. This risk is avoided if she receives artificial insemination from an Rh negative man.

More and more single women opt for artificial insemination—usually career women in their thirties who wish to have a child before they reach the age when that is risky or impossible. Some specialists estimate that 10 percent of all the women now pregnant from artificial insemination are single and living alone.

In July 1980, what was probably the first artificial insemination lawsuit brought by a single woman was filed by Mary Ann Smedes, thirty-six, of East Detroit, Michigan. The defendant, Wayne State University's Mott Center, had refused to allow the woman to be artificially inseminated because they have an "unwritten policy" of limiting artificial insemination to married women. The suit was brought because Smedes believed her constitutional rights were being violated and also as a challenge to the presumption that unmarried women are not fit for parenthood. The outcome was still pending at this writing.

However, the greatest number of patients are still those whose husbands cannot father a child. Researchers note that the sperm count of the average American male is falling.

Why?

Stress and life-style have been determined as the causes by science.

Smoking—regular cigarettes or marijuana—will lower a man's sperm count, as will excessive alcohol or working long hours at a desk job where there are many pressures. Even the wearing of tight-fitting clothing, such as designer jeans, can have an adverse affect on a male's sperm count. When we take into consideration the large number of men who meet these symptoms, we can understand the growth of sperm banks in recent years.

There are two ways to secure artificial insemination. A private physician or gynecologist may be consulted, or the would-be parents can go to a sperm bank that provides both the semen and a physician. A private doctor usually obtains the sperm from medical students, because they are young, have above-average intelligence, and are readily available.

The sperm bank employs students and men carefully selected for both intelligence and appearance, and will conduct a careful medical check to make sure there are no genetic defects or other negative hereditary characteristics. The deciding factor, however, is the sperm count in the semen. Today, the average American male has 60 million mobile sperm per milliliter of semen. Sperm banks insist that their donors have 130 million per milliliter. There will some loss during storage, so the initial count must be extremely high.

Some men pay a sperm bank to store their own semen for future use. Perhaps they are about to undergo a vasectomy but want to retain the option of having a child at a later date. Or, working in jobs which require them to be near high levels of radiation, they may be fearful of genetic damage or physical damage to the reproductive system and want samples of their semen as insurance. These samples of private sperm are never given to patients without the approval of the donor. Neither is semen of a person known to either the woman or her husband.

The reason for this is that anonymity must be preserved. Unlike adoptive parents, who often make a point of telling children they are adopted, few parents of an artifical insemination child wish him to know the truth. Also, when the donor knows the family, psychological changes may occur as he sees another man raising "his" child. This is another reason to go to a sperm bank rather than to a private physician, for sperm banks can guarantee privacy much better than a doctor.

Sperm banks can also match the donor's physical traits more closely to that of the man who will be the legal parent. In fact, when the child is born, friends often comment about how much he or she looks like the legal father. And should the parents wish to have additional children through artificial insemination, a sperm bank is more likely to have other samples of the same donor's sperm. Therefore, the children will be true siblings.

When the donor comes to the sperm bank to donate his semen, he must have abstained from sex for at least forty-eight hours. He is led to a private room containing a reclining chair and magazines with erotic photographs. The man ejaculates into a container and immediately brings the sample to a lab technician, who does an analysis and prepares the sample for storage. If the ejaculate is acceptable, the donor is paid approximately twenty-five dollars. Some men have earned their college education by delivering sperm samples every three days.

The sperm specimen is placed in a straw—white for Caucasians and blue for blacks—and frozen in liquid nitrogen at a temperature of −196 degrees Celsius, just like corneal transplants. But unlike other stored tissue, frozen sperm can survive for an indefinite period. Recently a woman in Detroit, Michigan, gave birth to a child from ten-year-old sperm. But some sperm are destroyed during the freezing and thawing process, and the effectiveness of frozen sperm is less than that of a sample that is immediately inseminated without freezing. Fresh sperm does begin to lose its mobility if not used within two hours of ejaculation, but doctors usually meet that deadline. Fresh sperm is also able to live in the female reproductive tract for up to seventy-two hours, whereas frozen sperm usually dies within a day. Most physicians believe that fresh semen causes pregnancy sooner in a recipient and without the necessity of repeated insemination, as is often needed with frozen sperm. ·

The process by which the recipient receives the sperm is relatively painless. A doctor injects the semen into the cervix. Usually two or three inseminations are performed during one ovulation cycle. At times fertilization occurs after the first series, but as a rule three cycle attempts must be conducted. In some cases dozens of inseminations are needed before the women becomes pregnant. At the present time, costs range from $150 to $400 per month.

Perhaps the most remarkable aspect of sperm banking is that those couples who have a child through the insemination process are more likely to remain happily married than couples who have children through the normal methods. The parents of a sperm-bank child explain this by saying their child was wanted, whereas another youngster might have arrived unexpectedly. And, on a more philosophical level, the parents of an artifical insemination child say that the child is a statement of the parents' spiritual union rather than merely their physical capabilities.

Three

IMPLANTS

In a way, medical science has come full circle. From ancient times until a few years ago, transplanted organs were only a dream, and doctors could only restore limited function with artificial body parts such as wooden limbs. Then, as doctors began to discover ways of transplanting organs from one person to another, this seemed to be the miracle cure of the future. But the rejection syndrome, which still thwarts complete success, has sent other researchers back to artifical organs.

Today, many people believe the future will see a much wider use of artificial organs—especially those made from a combination of natural and manufactured materials—than of actual organs. And, indeed, many of the newer spare body parts, which are made from a synthetic material that prevents rejection plus natural cells or tissue, seem to be highly succesful in duplicating the actual organ.

THE ARTIFICIAL BLADDER

To say that scientists have developed an *artificial* bladder is misleading. What has been developed is the use of nonhuman organic tissue to help a damaged or diseased bladder move through the normal healing process. The bladder is an organ vital to the proper function of the body, because it is here that urine collects before being discharged from the system. If injury or damage has affected the bladder, the release of urine may be halted or occur too frequently.

Fortunately, the bladder is highly regenerative, which means it repairs itself with new cellular growth. But often the organ needs to be helped while it is undergoing that recovery. Scientists at the Department of Artificial Organs at the Cleveland Clinic Foundation have been working to discover a material that can be used to reconstruct a bladder. The problem was that this unknown substance would have to dissolve slowly as the organ itself produced new tissue. Today they believe the breakthrough has been accomplished.

The experiments were conducted first on dogs. Using pericardium, the membranous sac that surrounds a cow's heart, they treated the tissue chemically and then placed the material into the wall of a dog's bladder. In the following weeks and months, the researchers were delighted to see that, as the dog's bladder healed, the pericardium steadily dissolved and finally disappeared. Encouraged by success with animals, doctors used the new technique on five human volunteers. Although it is still too soon to gauge long-range results, the five people were still well one year later.

Obviously, more research will have to be completed on this method of helping the bladder recover before it can be declared usable and safe for patients in general. We can be optimistic, however, that this intriguing new way of helping the body heal itself has a big future.

ARTIFICIAL BLOOD

Blood is perhaps the most underestimated part of our body. It fights disease and carries oxygen to the cells and carbon dioxide to the lungs, where it is expelled. Blood also carries vitamins to the tissues. Thus, it is truly our lifeline. The composition of human blood is extremely complex. The numerous small components serve so many specialized functions that the exact duplication of normal blood by an artificial material is still impossible.

Dr. Gottfried Schmer of the University of Washington, Seattle, has developed a means of rebuilding red blood cells from old cells. He drains the contents of the old cell, leaving behind the empty "ghost membrane sac," which is then refilled with new chemicals. According to Schmer, these reconstructed cells can be gathered together, pressed into a gel, and then set in a semipermeable cartridge. Custom-designed organs might be produced from such cartridges. Although these semiartificial organs are not yet in a state where they can be tested, Dr. Schmer has designed an artificial kidney, using his rebuilt red blood cells.

Additional research has been conducted in the United States and in Japan on producing something that can be used for human blood temporarily, such as during operations, where large quantities of whole blood for transfusions cannot be obtained. Both American and Japanese scientists worked with a preparation that utilized liquid fluorocarbons or chemical combinations of fluorine and carbon. The reason for using these compounds was that they can absorb and carry oxygen and carbon dioxide just as natural blood does within our body.

Family Health magazine announced in March 1980 that such a product was now available. Fluosol, a petroleum-based chemical, had been successfully tested on fifty-five patients in Japan and is now available for *emergency* cases in the United States. For example, the first three Americans to receive Fluosol during an operation were Jehovah's Witnesses, who, for religious reasons, could not accept transfusions of normal blood. The artificial blood, while not as miraculous as the natural material, is truly amazing.

A strong motivation for developing Fluosol was the high incidence of hepatitis resulting from the regular transfusions. In Japan, there is an 80 percent risk of contracting hepatitis when receiving blood from a donor. The rate is not as staggering in the United States, but Americans spend approximately $86 million each year to cure hepatitis that has developed from donations of blood. Artificial blood eliminates the danger of disease transmission.

There are other advantages to artificial blood. First, although its functions are more limited than those of real blood, the jobs are handled better. Artificial blood carries three times as much oxygen as natural blood. Also, when administering Fluosol, there is no need to match blood types of donor and recipient because the substance is compatible with all types—even the rarest forms of blood. Artificial blood is also biologically inert, which means it does not react with other substances in the body or form compounds that have to be filtered from the bloodstream by the liver and the kidneys.

Patients who cannot receive normal blood transfusions may be aided by Fluosol or other artificial blood. For example, in burn victims and people suffering from shock, capillaries become constricted, limiting the blood flow.

Since a Fluosol molecule is only 1/10 the size of a red blood cell, the artificial blood can still move through the narrowed passageways. Also, certain types of cancer patients may be treated more effectively if artificial blood can replace their natural blood temporarily. The reason is that some drugs used to treat cancer react negatively when they come in contact with blood proteins. Fluosol does not contain these proteins.

Surprisingly, the medical wonder is less expensive than the regular blood used for transfusions. At the present, Fluosol is about a quarter the cost of human blood or $15 per half-liter. Making artificial blood even more attractive is the fact that artificial blood can be stored frozen for approximately three years, thus allowing stockpiles to be set aside for emergencies. Fluosol, and other artificial bloods which may be produced in the future, will probably never equal natural blood in its many versatile qualities. However, these manufactured materials will save lives and make other medical advances possible.

ARTIFICIAL BRAIN PACEMAKER

The human brain is, of course, much too complicated and serves too many functions for scientists even to contemplate an artificial substitute. In fact, much information remains to be learned about how the brain actually works. However, as you will discover in this section of the book, scientists have made a new use of an old technique—discharging an electrical current into the brain. This has long been a method of behavior modification in laboratory tests on animals, but only recently have researchers begun experimenting with this principle in hopes of developing artificial body parts.

One such device has been developed to help an emotionally disturbed person by discharging a low-level electric current into portions of the brain—a brain pacemaker. Dr. Robert Heath of Tulane University, Louisiana, is the inventor of this contrivance, still in the testing stage. The brain pacemaker is used with severely neurotic and schizophrenic patients. An opening is made in the back of the skull, and the pacemaker, which consists of three to five metal electrodes, is set on the brain's surface. There is no sensation of pain for the wearer because the brain is incapable of feeling pain, but the electrical discharge alters feelings of depression or hostility in the patient.

Further on, you will be reading how scientists are using similar techniques to help the blind to see and the deaf to hear.

ARTIFICIAL CARTILAGE AND JOINTS

For minor replacements of tendons and cartilage and more major body parts such as wrists and knees, a number of synthetic materials are available to surgeons. An artificial tendon is being tested by the U.S. Army Institute of Surgical Research, utilizing Dacron tape, coated with Silastic. Finger joints can be replaced with flexible silicone rubber, allowing great mobility. Artificial wrists with flexibility equal to human wrists can be implanted, and a total knee replacement has been developed at the University of Michigan. The artificial knee is constructed from a metal alloy and bends the way a natural knee moves. For reconstructing noses and chins, a substance is applied externally. The material is soft and almost matches the normal skin in appearance. All these artificial body parts have been developed and tested, and most are regularly used on patients today.

Perhaps the most famous joint replacement is the artificial hip. To understand the need for a total hip replacement, it is necessary to know how the natural hip works.

The hip is actually a ball-and-socket joint. The head of the long thigh bone, or femur, is rounded like a ball and fits into a cartilage-lined hollow in the hipbone. The ball and socket are lubricated by the natural synovial fluid that bathes the body's joints, thus allowing the femur bone to swivel easily in its hipbone cavity.

If arthritis strikes the hip joint or a serious bone fracture at the site fails to heal correctly, painful crippling may result. Formerly, the method of treatment was to attach an artificial head to the femur or reshape and reline the socket. Unfortunately, the natural fluids did not always keep the artificial parts oiled, and every step was agony for the patient. In 1954, a forty-two-year-old English surgeon started work on a means whereby patients with painful hip problems could not only find relief but regain lost mobility.

Dr. John Charnley began his hip research soon after World War II. At the Manchester Royal Infirmary, England, he developed new methods of hip surgery and later transferred his studies to the now world-famous Centre for Hip Surgery, which he established at Wrightington Hospital in Wigan. In 1954, a patient came to Dr. Charnley with an embarrassing hip problem. In an earlier operation, an acrylic head had been attached to his thigh bone, which worked very well but squeaked audibly. The man's wife refused to dine out with him because the noise attracted so much attention. Dr. Charnley built an artificial joint that had a stainless-steel ball, which fit into a socket of Teflon, the most friction-free material then known. When installed—not only in the patient with the noise problem, but other sufferers—Charnley's hip yielded amazing results. Gone were the pain and inability to walk which had characterized the patients' lives until the operation.

Word spread quickly about the new artificial hip, and within a year Charnley performed approximately 300 operations. But by the end of the first year, concrete evidence existed that the hip replacement was not as successful as first thought. Discomfort and, in most cases, pain returned as severe as before the replacement. The problem was that the Teflon in the hipbone cup wore away.

As Charnley contemplated the situation and weighed the possiblity of a sealed-bearing type of hip, sheer luck was to provide the answer. A salesman showed Charnley samples of a high-density polyethylene. The poor lasting power of Teflon had convinced Charnley that he had to avoid synthetic materials, so he told an assistant to deposit the sample in the trash barrel. Fortunately, the assistant decided to test the polyethylene on a machine they had used to determine the wear-resistance ability of other materials. The results were unbelievable. After three weeks on the apparatus, the polyethylene had not worn away as much as the Teflon had in only twenty-four hours. There were other bonuses with this high-density new material. The substance had a surface that was less slippery than Teflon, which indicated that the polyethylene would restrict movement, but it had something Teflon lacked: it could be lubricated by the normal body fluid, and this would obviate friction in nature's own way.

In November 1962, John Charnley began using the high-density polyethylene in his artificial hip replacements. But his unfortunate experience with Teflon had taught him caution. Now he built an X-ray marker into his hip replacements—a metal wire the exact diameter of the plastic socket. This enabled him to monitor how well the polyethylene was lasting after being installed. The wearing factor of the new substance proved to be excellent. In ten years, the average wear was only 1.5 millimeters, and about 10 percent of the hip replacements showed no deterioration at all.

As for mobility, patients with polyethylene hip replacements have had no difficulty with this at all. The only restriction placed on them is that they avoid contact sports.

Otherwise, they swim, play tennis, and even hike in rugged terrain.

Hospitals and medical centers throughout Great Britain and now the world use Charnley's operation technique, called low-friction arthroplasty. Even in some cases where cancer has developed in the general area of the joint, a replacement can be carried out. But every sufferer of hip problems is not eligible for a replacement. As with any operation, the surgeon must consider many factors, such as the general physical and emotional health of the patient and the condition of the bones to which artificial parts will be fastened. The two most common problems that prevent a patient from receiving the artificial hip are obesity and chronic infection of the hip joint.

The operation is usually simple (depending, of course, on the particular patient's affliction), and the time required can be as short as fifty minutes or as long as three hours. An incision is made lengthwise on the hip and thigh. The surgeon moves the muscles aside, revealing the hip joint. The ball on the thigh bone is sawed free, and the socket in the hipbone is cleaned and reshaped. Now the artificial parts are attached. An acrylic paste is applied to the new socket—Charnley's technique is to use large amounts of paste, whereas other surgeons spread only a thin layer—then the socket is set into the hipbone. The marrow is removed from the cut end of the thigh bone, paste is applied, and the stainless-steel ball piece is inserted into the socket in the thigh bone.

In most cases, the patient is on his feet after four or five days, but very little weight is placed on the new hip. Two to three weeks later, the patient returns home, and after approximately three months he usually no longer needs a cane. The success rate for the artificial hip operation is more than 95 percent, a high figure indeed when evaluating transplanted or artificial organs.

As positive as the results are with John Charnley's artificial hip, improvements are still being sought. Researchers at the University of Wisconsin are attempting to develop a material that will be as strong and resilient as the stainless-steel piece now used, but lighter. Bones would be constructed from metal powder, the ends highly polished to allow easy movement, but the remainder of the synthetic bones left porous. That way, scientists hope the natural bone will grow into the artificial bone, anchoring it into place. Only preliminary tests of this new technique have been conducted up to this writing.

Whatever the results of the new experiments, the astounding success of Dr. John Charnley's artificial hip has earned it a high reputation in the realm of artificial body parts.

ARTIFICIAL EYE

A true artificial eye—that is, one that will restore some measure of vision—has not yet been perfected but major steps have been taken in that direction. People who have been blind for years have been enabled to see points of light, geometric shapes, and even Braille letters transmuted into "visual" images.

The beginnings of this artificial eye occurred in 1968 when Dr. William Dobelle read a scientific paper published by two English scientists. Giles Brindley and Walpole Lewin had managed to make a blind woman see a tiny point of light by touching the exposed part of her visual cortex with electrified wires. The visual cortex is the "vision center" of the brain. Since the brain does not experience pain, the woman was able to remain awake during the experiment and report the results. Although a small point of light is far from a total image, Brindley and Lewin were excited about the potential use of this in aiding blind people. Naming these points of light phosphenes (a word already in existence), meaning "an afterimage or excitation of the retina by some cause other than light," the two scientists published the results of their experiment. However, the scientific world believed the theory was without value.

Dr. William Dobelle reasoned that if you could produce a mosaic of phosphenes, blind people might well be able to see. In 1969, Dobelle formed a research team with a University of Utah colleague, Michael Mladejovsky. Dr. Mladejovsky designed the computer and electrodes they would use in their experiments, and Dobelle, the biophysicist and neurophysiologist, would determine what was needed and how to install the gear inside the human body.

First, however, more information had to be garnered about phosphenes. Other questions also demanded answers. If they achieved their dream and were able to make a blind person see again by a steady but weak electrical current in the brain, what would be the long-term effects on that individual's brain? Also, since electronic vision would mean implanting apparatus within the skull, what materials would best withstand chemical reaction with substances in the human body?

Dobelle and his team conducted thirty-seven experiments. Their first problem was to gain access to exposed visual cortices in living patients. Surgeons in the United States and Canada were urged to contact Dobelle if a patient of theirs faced an operation for a brain tumor near the visual cortex. While the brain was exposed during the operation, Dobelle would conduct his experiments. Offers of doctors and their patients to volunteer for this experiment began rolling into Dobelle's office. Dobelle and his team set to work. Even though the patients had vision, they experienced a point of light when an electrode touched the visual cortex. The results were encouraging and useful. One electrode produced one phosphene in each eye. Would increasing the number of electrodes increase the number of phosphenes? Yes. Also, the brightness of the light was greater when the strength of the electrical current was stronger. Luckily, there was no debilitating effect over a long period of time. After all, the brain receives electrical impulses from the nervous system every moment of the day.

By 1975, Dobelle and Mladejovsky prepared for their next big experiment—installing their electronic package inside a human volunteer. They had worked toward this step by meeting weekly with a group of blind volunteers and briefing them on the progress of the research team. A member of this group, Craig, had been blinded in a shooting accident in 1963. Although he realized that the package placed in his skull would not give him true vision, Craig agreed to be the guinea pig.

A square Teflon ribbon studded with sixty-four platinum electrodes was placed inside his skull and pressed against the visual cortex. Sixty-four wires led from it, under his scalp, to a spot above his right ear. Here the wires were connected to a round black graphite socket the size of a dime. Now, a few days each month, Craig boards a plane and flies from Salt Lake City, Utah, to New York City and the Columbia Presbyterian Medical Center, where a computer is plugged into the socket. When a weak electrical signal passes from the computer to the Teflon patch, Craig sees bluish-white lights. The computer has been able to make Craig see triangles and a simple white line on a dark background. When the research team wanted to show letters, they realized that sixty-four phosphenes were not enough to form the letters of the alphabet. Craig, however, had learned to read Braille, and Braille letters can be constructed from variations of six points of light. Thus, he has been able to read sentences fed to him by the computer.

When interviewed for an article in *New York* magazine in the fall of 1979, Dr. William Dobelle was asked how seeing with these phosphenes would appear visually. Dobelle

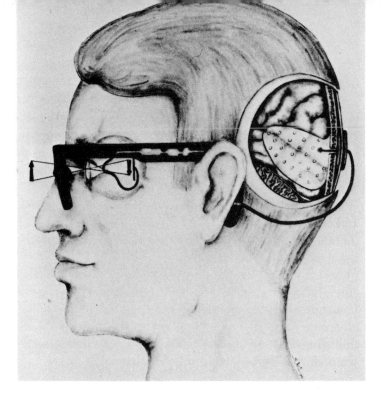

The proposed artificial eye would have a small television camera in the eye socket. The glasses would contain a microprocessor that sends the pattern to the electrodes imbedded under the skull.

DIVISION OF ARTIFICIAL ORGANS—UNIVERSITY OF UTAH

compared it to the images on an animated electronic billboard or "like the scoreboard at Yankee Stadium."

And what is the ultimate goal of Craig's system? First, a Teflon strip would be set in both sides of the head. Each would be equipped with 256 electrodes. An artificial eye containing a miniature television camera would be placed in one socket. The artificial eye would be connected to the natural eye muscles so the eye would have the mobility of a normal one. The television camera would pick up images and send them to a computer built into a dummy eyeglass frame. The eyeglass frame will also hold the battery pack to supply power for the unit. As the images come into the computer, the device then sends the proper phosphene translations through a plug in the skull such as Craig now wears. The 256-electrode system on each side of the visual cortex then emits the proper electrical messages so the person will have sight flashed on the retina.

How much will a patient have to pay for this electronic vision system or artificial eye? Dr. Dobelle figures between $3,000 and $5,000 for the hardware and approximately the same amount for medical costs.

A hefty price, yes, but not when weighed against what the blind person will be buying—sight. Initial experiments have already been completed in setting the minute television cameras into some patients' eyes. While this project is being brought to completion, Dr. William Dobelle is working on his next goal—electronic hearing.

ARTIFICIAL HEARING

Most people know that sound is caused by vibrations. For example, if we take a spoon and bang it against a pot, the metal rattles, sending vibrations through the air molecules. These vibrating molecules set other molecules into action, and so the sound is transmitted to our ears. The human ear—though small in size—is a highly complex unit, for its job is to change the vibrations to fluid pressure waves and finally into electrical impulses. Indeed the organ is so complicated that even to consider an ear transplant at this time is impossible. A look at how vibrations eventually become "sounds" will explain why.

The auricle, or outer part of the ear, is merely there to collect the sound vibrations. We can extend its function by cupping a hand around it, thus capturing still more vibrations and increasing the volume. The vibrations enter the outer ear, traveling along the auditory canal until they strike the eardrum, which in turn vibrates. On the opposite side of the eardrum is the middle ear, where three bones— called the hammer, the anvil, and the stirrup—are connected by ligaments. Think of a blacksmith striking a hammer on an anvil to make a stirrup. In the same way, the vibrating eardrum activates the hammer bone, which moves the anvil, and the vibrations are passed along to the stirrup.

In this last step, the three bones, moving in unison, magnify the vibrations, much the way a fulcrum increases the force applied at one end of a lever. As the stirrup bone pushes on the oval window (inner wall of the middle ear), the vibrations have been increased twenty-two times.

On the other side of the oval window, the vibrations enter the snail-shaped cochlea located in the inner ear— the third part of the ear. The vibrations pass through the fluid in the cochlea, causing "waves" to ripple along the basilar membrane of the cochlea. The rods of Corti rest on the basilar membrane and contain 23,500 hair cells with soft hairs that are attached to another membrane—the tectorial membrane. The basilar fibers of the cochlea, moving in fluid waves, shake these hair cells, making them bend back and forth. This action creates electrical impulses, which are detected by the nerve fibers at the base of the hair cells. These nerve fibers, joining to form the auditory nerve, carry the electrical signals to the auditory cortex of the brain. In some way (scientists are not certain exactly how), the brain absorbs the impulses from the auditory nerve and registers them as sound.

Because our hearing system has so many component parts, hearing loss can be caused by any one of a number of malfunctions. From the eardrum to the auditory nerve, the route of the vibrations, fluid waves, or electrical charges can be blocked at any one point, and the brain will receive no message. Hearing loss can be described in two ways: severity and type.

In terms of *severity*, there are many people who are not even aware that they suffer from a loss of hearing. A slight loss of perception of high-pitched sounds merely muffles the shrillness of the world around us. Hard-of-hearing persons have an impairment severe enough so that they have trouble understanding ordinary conversation. Total deafness means that absolutely no sounds can be heard; even the strongest hearing aid, say, cannot assist these people.

There are two *types* of hearing loss: conduction deafness and nerve or perception deafness. The word "conduction" explains well that kind of hearing loss. Something is blocking the conduction of the vibrations. Therefore, the problem is generally in the middle ear. Infections may have damaged delicate structures there or the bones may be malformed at birth. Generally, victims of conduction deafness can be helped with artificial hearing devices or by surgery. Nerve deafness can be minor—a loss of high-pitched sounds, while good hearing remains in the lower-pitched regions—or severe. If extensive nerve damage has occured, the condition is never repairable.

For years, the hearing aid has been a familiar sight to many people. At first, aids were bulky devices, drawing attention to their wearers, and some people with a hearing loss preferred to tune out the world rather than announce their disability to everyone. However, with the coming of transistors, portable radios shrank to the size of a deck of cards, and so did hearing aids. Today, they are not only much smaller, but more powerful than their ancestors.

One type of hearing aid is a small button worn in the better-hearing ear; it contains a receiver that captures the sound and amplifies the vibrations. Another kind of hearing aid is fitted into an eyeglass frame with a barely visible plastic tube leading into the ear. An even stronger hearing aid is worn behind the ear; the unit contains a receiver, which detects the sounds, a microphone, and an amplifier to increase the intensity of the vibrations entering the outer ear. The most powerful assistance device is the "body aid." Everything about the body aid is large and strong so it must be carried in a case or strapped to the chest. A cord connects the case to the ear. If the hearing loss is severe enough and suited to this technique, the patient might even wear a unit in each ear.

As effective as contemporary hearing aids are, they cannot help a person who has suffered an injury or disease resulting in total deafness. But there are "helpers" for those with complete disability, devices that assist in making their daily lives more convenient and safer. Most of these consist of sound-sensitive apparatus, which change sound into another medium—turning the doorbell's ring into a blinking light, switching on a light when the phone rings, waking a sleeper by vibrating under his pillow. The Silent Pager is a device that enables parents of deaf children to contact their youngsters; the parent dials a special number, and the Pager sends out a series of silent vibrations, which are received by a unit carried by the deaf child.

One of the newest means of helping deaf people is a method borrowed from the blind: the hearing dog. The American Humane Association of Denver, Colorado, trains dogs to detect sound and react in various ways. Each dog is trained to help a specific person, because deaf people have varying needs. A deaf mother might need a hearing dog to alert her that her baby is crying, whereas an elderly person living alone in an apartment might require a dog who can warn him that the smoke alarm is buzzing. Dogs can be taught to react to a variety of household sounds: telephones, doorbells, knocks on the door, a particular voice, or even the sound of another pet. Upon hearing the sound, the dog runs to the deaf person, nuzzles him, and then runs over to the origin of the sound. If the deaf person does not react, the dog repeats the process until his owner responds to whatever is making the noise.

One technique, closely allied to similar work in helping the blind, is electronic hearing. Almost twenty-five years ago, Dr. William House, a researcher at the Los Angeles Foundation of Otology, today called the Ear Research Institute, was shown an article on French experiments in the use of electrical impulses on the ear's nervous system. Until that time, very little medical work had touched on the inner ear, for fear of obliterating any potential of that very delicate area to transmit sound. However, intrigued by the article, House began careful experiments on animals and then human volunteers to see if there was an avenue to

Dr. William F. House, the researcher who developed electronic hearing.

EAR RESEARCH INSTITUTE

Charles A. Graser, the first recipient of Dr. House's electronic hearing apparatus.

electronic hearing. The first crude model was inserted in a patient in 1970.

Charles Graser had been a California schoolteacher, who drove tanker trucks on weekends for extra earnings. In 1959, a truck that he was refueling exploded, and the fire severely burned him. Rushed to the hospital, Graser received emergency treatment, including large doses of streptomycin to prevent the infection that can strike burn victims so quickly. The antibiotic did prevent infection, but the massive amounts destroyed the hair cells in his inner ear. As explained, these cells are needed to activate the fine hairs in the rods of Corti, which in turn excite the nerve fibers near the hair cells. Auditory messages reaching Graser's inner ear never became electrical signals to be carried along the auditory nerve.

To install the electronic ear, surgeons had to drill through the hardest bone in the human body—the mastoid bone behind the right and left ears. By doing so, they gained access to the spiral-shaped cochlea. There, they implanted six threadlike electrodes with minute platinum balls on their tips. Wires ran from the electrodes to a small plug imbedded in the skin behind Graser's right ear. But there was more to this new form of artificial hearing. Graser was given an eyeglass frame with a tiny transmitter in the tip of the right earpiece. A cord ran from this transmitter to a battery-powered transmitter strapped to the patient's chest. Sounds were picked up by the transmitter and sent along the wire to the transmitter in the eyeglass frame. There, the sounds were beamed to the induction coil behind the right ear. The coil brought them to the electrodes planted in the cochlea. Now the nerve fibers could be set into action, and the electrical impulses were on their way along the auditory nerve to the brain.

The electronic ear has had a certain degree of success. Graser, for the first time in years, could hear sounds like school bells, a cat meowing, and even bacon frying. The major weakness of the cochlea implant is that the device is unable to make human speech understandable. The pitch changes are much too subtle to be carried through the electronic hearing system. However, the vocal sounds that are transmitted help the wearer to read lips more successfully.

Dr. William Dobelle, the artificial-eye man, is now working to improve House's method of implanting electrodes on the cochlea. As sounds travel through the spiraling cochlea, they change. So, if Dobelle can determine the best patterns of stimulation for the electrodes, the deaf patient might eventually understand human speech.

70

"Walter Cronkite might sound like Donald Duck," Dobelle admitted in *New York* magazine on October 22, 1979, "but at least he'll be understandable."

Dobelle and his team are experimenting with electrical stimulation of the auditory cortex, the hearing center of the brain. Dobelle and Dr. Michael Mladejovsky have learned that, when deaf persons have their auditory cortex excited by one electrode, they hear a sound. For these, they adopted the arbitrary term *audenes*. When scientists are able to make these audenes form patterns, as they did with phosphenes, another form of electronic hearing will be possible.

Work continues today on perfecting electronic hearing. Experiments are being conducted at the University of Utah Medical Center under the direction of Dr. Donald Eddington.

DIVISION OF ARTIFICIAL ORGANS—UNIVERSITY OF UTAH

ARTIFICIAL HEART AND
CIRCULATORY SYSTEM PARTS

1. *Artificial Arteries and Veins*

In the early 1950's, Dr. Michael E. DeBakey of the Baylor College of Medicine devised a means whereby veins and arteries could be constructed from man-made material. When he was dissatisfied with the materials available in the hospital supply room, he went shopping in a Houston, Texas, department store. There, he purchased swatches of cloth—nylon, cotton, Dacron, and Orlon. Employing his wife's sewing machine, he made tubes from each type of fabric and tested the tubes in experiments with dogs. Of the four fabrics, he learned that Dacron worked best.

Today, large arteries can be replaced by tubes of woven Dacron. A problem arises, however with smaller synthetic tubes for the circulatory system, because the blood flowing through them clots, halting the blood's movement through the body. Dr. Donald Lyman of the University of Utah, has devised a new polymer for making smaller artificial blood vessels, less than six millimeters thick. If his experiments prove successful, then this material can be used to replace arteries in the kidney, liver, lower leg, or the brain.

2. *Heart Valves*

To understand the vital function of the heart valves, we must return to the functioning of the heart itself. We have already seen how blood is pumped *into* the heart by way of the atria and *out* through the ventricles. This movement of the blood through the heart is facilitated by the fact that both right and left atria contract at the same time and then both ventricles do the same.

The right atrium fills with blood, which is returning from the body and contains waste products, while the left atrium collects the blood as it comes back from the lungs, where it was cleansed of carbon dioxide. Thus both atria are mo-

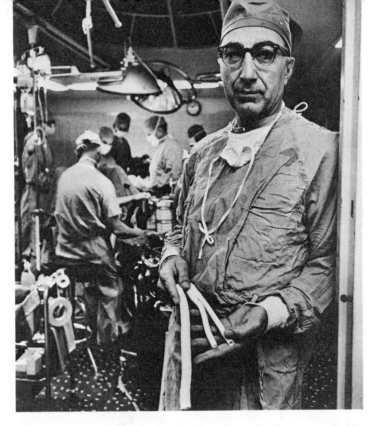

Dr. Michael DeBakey, who developed artificial arteries, holds several Dacron arterial grafts.

mentarily gorged. Then both atria contract, sending the blood into the ventricles below them. As the ventricles contract, the right pushes the "dirty" blood to the lungs, and the left sends the "clean" blood into the aorta, whence it will flow to all parts of the body.

Four valves control the flow of blood during this pumping operation. As the blood moves from the right atrium into the right ventricle, it passes through the *tricuspid* valve, which has three triangular-shaped leaflets. On the left side, as the blood passes from the left atrium into the left ventricle, it moves through the *mitral* valve, so called

73

because its two peaked flaps resemble a bishop's miter, or tall pointed headpiece. These two valves, mitral and tricuspid, are called the atrioventricular or AV valves. As the ventricles contract, the AV valves must close to prevent a backward flow of the blood. Simultaneously, two valves in the ventricles must open to permit the blood to escape from the heart. On the right, the *pulmonary* valve permits the blood to move into the pulmonary artery toward the lungs, while on the left, the *aorta* valve lets the blood flow into the aorta artery. These two valves, called the *semilunar* valves, must also close as the ventricles relax to block a backward movement of the pumped blood.

The sound of the closing valves is what makes up the two thumps of your heartbeat. People in medicine refer to the "lub-dub" sound of the heart. The lower-pitched "lub" is the sound of the AV valves closing, while the higher-pitched "dub" is the sound of the semilunar valves in the ventricles snapping shut.

Diseases such as syphilis or rheumatic fever can damage the heart valves or cause scar tissue to grow around them so they fail to work properly. Either the valves do not permit enough blood to flow through the heart or else they do not close properly, and there is blood seepage. Faulty heart valves must often be replaced, or eventually heart failure will occur.

Although valve transplant operations can be done, there are simply not enough natural heart valves available, no matter how effectively medical centers work to procure them. Donald Longmore in his book, *Spare-Part Surgery*, discusses how a hospital in England "collects hearts removed during routine necropsies (autopsies) all over London; our weekly intake averages seven hearts. A few may already have begun to putrefy, and these we discard." They also do not use any that show congenital defects or have sites where clots might form. The valves are tested by pouring saline solution into the heart. Those that pass are then routinely used for valve replacement.

But that's just one hospital. Elsewhere there is a shortage of natural heart valves, aggravated by the fact that the donor's valves must match the recipient's in size and shape. An artificial valve seemed to be the answer.

In 1952, Dr. Charles A. Hufnagel of Georgetown University, Washington, D.C., invented and implanted the first artificial valve, a plastic ball encased in a metal socket. This Hufnagel valve was sewn into the aortic artery to replace a patient's defective aortic valve. However, as the use of the Hufnagel heart valve increased, an unexpected side effect was discovered. Normally, physicians need a stethoscope to hear the closing of the heart valves. But

Artificial mitral and aortic heart valves. The base is knitted Teflon, and the plastic ball is in a cage of stainless alloy.

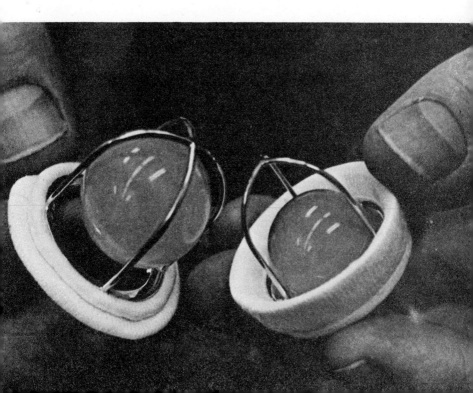

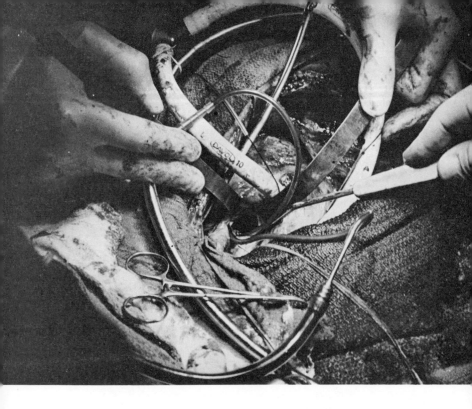

A defective aortic valve has been trimmed from the heart. The hole into the heart, exposed by the surgeon's retractors, is nearly ready to receive its artificial valve.

when the Hufnagel ball snapped closed, a popping sound was audible without a stethoscope. If the wearer opened his mouth, the noise level increased, and people nearby could hear the clicking.

Fortunately, the Hufnagel valve was improved, and others like the Star-Edwards valve developed so that the noise problem was eliminated. Today, it is not unusual to find a patient with two or even three heart valves replaced by manufactured valves. In addition, artificial heart valves are made from stainless steel, titanium, Dacron, and Silastic rubber. One of the most recent is a porcine heterograft.

The valves of a pig's heart are removed, sterilized, treated with chemicals, and stored for a period to be certain there has been no bacterial contamination. Then they are sewn to a Dacron-covered frame and surgically implanted.

Artificial heart valves have alleviated the problem of locating enough replacement valves, but their use has brought about other difficulties. Initially, recipients experienced blood clotting around the mechanical valve and had to take daily dosages of medicines designed to lower the clotting power of the blood. This procedure in turn produces other health dangers, chiefly the possibility of uncontrolled bleeding. One benefit of the pig's heart valve on a Dacron frame is that fewer clotting problems occur. As a rule, a patient needs to take medicine for only a period of six to eight weeks after the implant. The porcine valve also has less potential for mechanical failure than other techniques, since there are no movable parts.

Undoubtedly, new refinements will continue to be introduced into the artificial heart valves now in use. Even if occasional malfunctions occur in some artificial valves, they are doing a job the patient's natural valves can no longer handle—keeping the person alive.

3. *The Heart-Lung Machine*

Today, open-heart surgery is common, but until the 1950's, there was no possible way to conduct an operation on the heart. Doctors were able to stop a heart from beating so that it could be worked on, but that would halt the flow of blood to the brain, and an interruption of blood supply as short as three minutes can do irreparable damage. Therefore, a machine was needed to take over the heart's functions while the doctors performed their delicate surgery.

The story of the heart-lung machine begins in the 1930's with Dr. Alexis Carrel, who was the first person to experiment with organ transplants in the early 1900's. Joining

Carrel in his search for such a device was a world-famous aviator, whom few people connect with the field of medicine—Charles Lindbergh.

Lindbergh came to the Rockefeller Institute in New York City, where Carrel worked as a researcher, to learn why a family member could not receive an operation for a heart defect. He stayed and teamed up with Alexis Carrel to develop the needed apparatus—Carrel supplying the scientific knowledge while Lindbergh provided the mechanical know-how. The result was a machine that could *perfuse* an organ, mentioned earlier, and was able to handle several functions of the heart as well. In 1936, the Carrel-Lindbergh invention was displayed at an international science conference in Copenhagen, Denmark, where the two originators applied the name which holds today: the heart-lung machine. As a testimonial to its importance in the development of surgery, models of the Carrel-Lindbergh machine are on display at the Smithsonian Institution, Washington, D.C.

Meanwhile, Dr. John Gibbon, Jr., of the Jefferson Medical College in Philadelphia, Pennsylvania, was conducting his own experiments with a similar device. In 1934, he built a heart-lung machine which is closely related to present-day hardware. His first experiments with cats proved successful, so he moved on to more complicated research on dogs. In 1953, Dr. Gibbon became the first person to use a heart-lung machine during a successful operation on a human being. An eighteen-year-old girl needed a heart defect closed, so while Dr. Gibbon operated, a heart-lung machine maintained the girl's blood flow. Further improvements on the device were made by Dr. Michael E. DeBakey and Dr. Denton Cooley in Houston, Texas. The two men became the first surgeons to use a heart-lung machine on a large number of patients.

What is a heart-lung machine?

As the name implies, the machine takes over the functions of the heart and the lungs—of the heart by pumping blood through the body, and of the lungs by cleansing the blood of carbon dioxide and adding oxygen. Because the blood is rerouted around the heart and lungs, this is also known as a circulatory bypass. In addition, the machine lowers the temperature of the patient's body, thus slowing down his bodily functions and lowering his need for food and oxygen.

The most important part of the heart-lung machine is the oxygenator, for that is where the carbon dioxide is removed and the oxygen supplied to the blood. Until recently, heart-lung machines used an oxygenator that pumped oxygen bubbles through the blood. Although this did provide the needed oxygen, the bubbles made the blood foamy, and another step had to be added to the process: defoaming. Moreover, the excessive handling of the blood while in the heart-lung machine damaged the red blood cells, causing them to release hemoglobin—the part of the blood cell that carries iron—into the bloodstream. The kidneys had to work extra hard to filter out the hemoglobin. In addition, the manipulation of the blood weakened its ability to clot. As a result, a patient could remain on that type of heart-lung machine for only three or four hours.

Today, the oxygenator contains silicone-rubber membranes. The blood passes between the membranes, which are immersed in oxygen. Oxygen molecules seep through the membranes into the blood, while the carbon-dioxide molecules in the blood pass the opposite way through the membranes. Thus the blood is "fed" and "cleansed" at the same time. In effect, this machine is truly replacing the lungs, because the same process takes place in the air sacs of the lungs where oxygen and carbon dioxide simultane-

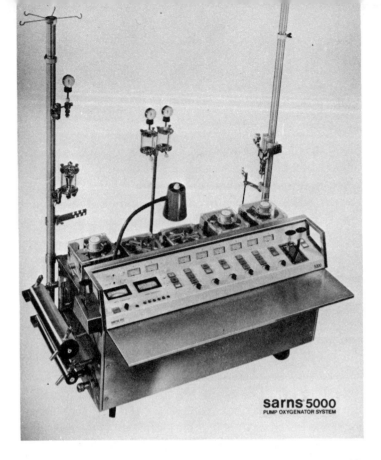

sarns 5000
PUMP OXYGENATOR SYSTEM

ously pass through the air-sac walls. Because there is much less blood damage in this new type of heart-lung machine, a patient can remain on it for several days.

This machine, which made possible Dr. Christiaan N. Barnard's famous heart transplants, is still undergoing improvements. Experiments are being conducted to see how the heart-lung machine may be used to aid patients with lung disease. If the machine can replace a person's heart during an operation, can it take over for the lungs during a recovery period, giving the patient's lungs time to rest and recover? Initial experiments seem to indicate a strong possibility that, yes, there is still another use for a machine that has already served thousands of people.

Implants

A modern model of the heart-lung machine that has made trans-planted and artificial body part operations a reality.

The working parts of a heart-lung machine.

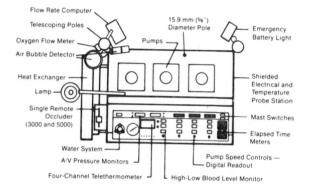

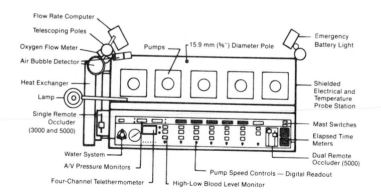

4. *The Left Ventricular Assist Device*

The dream of all researchers in the field of artificial body parts is the artificial heart. Research for this ultimate medical miracle has been in progress for decades. During the last fifteen years, the National Heart, Lung, and Blood Institute (NHLBI) has given grants amounting to over $50 million for the development of this artificial organ. To date, an artificial replacement for a faulty heart may indeed be close, rendered possible by something called a left ventricular assist device (LVAD).

What is an LVAD and how is it used?

The left ventricle is the portion of the heart that works hardest, because it pumps blood to all parts of the body except the lungs. Often a patient's heart needs time to gather strength after an operation, but until recently there was no way to allow the heart such rest. Leaving a patient for an extended period on a heart-lung machine caused blood damage. Too often, the end result was death.

In 1963, renowned heart specialist Dr. Michael De-Bakey was the first person to devise a mechanical means of bypassing the left ventricle. The device collected the blood that flows into the left atrium and pumped it directly into the aorta, so that the left ventricle did not have to work so hard. After a few hours or days of rest, the patients' own hearts were able to resume the full job of pushing the blood into the aorta.

Research in left ventricular assist devices has continued throughout the United States. In 1976, Dr. John Norman of the Texas Heart Institute (THI) perfected an LVAD that could be implanted directly in the patient. Dr. Norman's LVAD does not take blood from the left atrium as De-Bakey's pump did, but rather from the left ventricle itself. Otherwise, the principles of the two types are the same.

The LVAD is implanted in the patient's abdomen. The reason for this is that the chest is literally packed with important organs, which would have to be displaced to make room for the LVAD, and surgeons do not make incisions in the thoracic region unless it is ultranecessary. Operating on the abdomen is less risky, and there is more room for an LVAD. The hardware consists of an egg-shaped chamber approximately three inches long, containing three openings, two of which are regulated by valves. A tube is attached at one end to the bottom of the left ventricle and at the other to the top opening of the chamber. A second tube runs from the lower opening to the abdominal aorta. These two openings are controlled by valves. A third tube runs to an outside machine, the pump.

When the LVAD is in operation, the top valve opens, allowing blood to collect in a bladder within the chamber.

The portion of the LVAD which is imbedded in the patient's body.

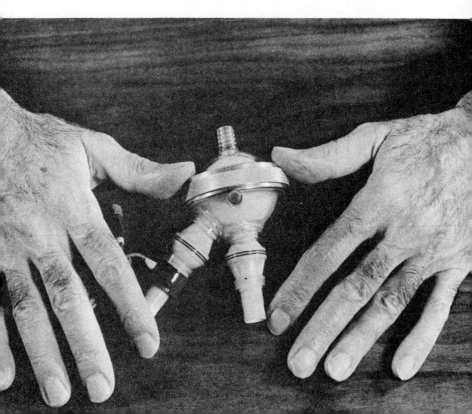

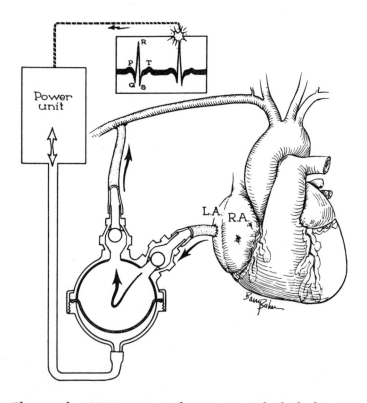

The complete LVAD circuit. The portion inside the body is attached to the heart as well as to an external power unit which controls its operation.

Then air is pumped into the LVAD, filling the space between the bladder and the outside walls. As the bladder is compressed by the building air pressure, the bottom valve opens, permitting the blood to flow into the abdominal aorta. Now the air is sucked from the chamber. The bottom valve closes, and the top valve opens, letting blood once again fill the bladder. During the time it took you to read this paragraph, that process would have happened many times, because the LVAD operates at the same rate as the patient's normal heartbeat.

Other LVADs work on the same principles. For example, a twenty-member team at Pennsylvania State University, headed by Dr. William S. Pierce, a surgeon, and two engineering professors, Drs. Winfred Phillips and John A. Brighton, worked seven years to design a different LVAD. Finally, in the summer of 1977, Pierce installed the LVAD in the body of a thirty-nine-year-old housewife, whose heart refused to start again after an operation on the valves. It was a resounding success. During her ninth day on the machine, the patient's heart was well enough to work unassisted, and several weeks later, she was discharged from the hospital.

The Penn State LVAD combined the methods used by Dr. DeBakey and those of the THI device. As in the THI machine, the blood was withdrawn from the left ventricle, but it was returned directly to the aorta near the heart as in DeBakey's ventricle bypass. The U-shaped tube, vaguely resembling a sink trap, had two hoses running from each tip of the U. One was attached to the base of the left ventricle, the other was sewn to the aorta. The extracorporeal machine was again an air pump. As in the THI artificial heart muscle, the machine alternately pumped and withdrew air. Circulating around a flexible polyurethane sac inside the tube, the air squeezed the sac and then permitted it to expand as new blood entered. The blood was drained from the heart and immediately returned to the bloodstream in the aorta at a normal heartbeat.

Equally successful was the device of a Swiss doctor, who recently kept a patient alive by hooking *two* ventricular assist pumps to the man's heart. It was this achievement that prompted Dr. Winfred Phillips of Penn State to comment that the realization of an artificial heart was nearly a reality.

In *New York* magazine on October 22, 1979, Dr. Phillips said that "the step from there to the artificial heart is not a giant one."

But what is contemplated for future LVADs before we have an artificial heart? Dr. Yukihiko Nose, a native of Hokkaido, Japan, who now heads the Department of Artificial Organs at the Cleveland Clinic Foundation, Ohio, may have an answer for that question. All LVADs in present use are temporary machines, designed to aid a heart until the natural organ has rebuilt its strength. But some patients require a full-time LVAD. Is there nothing for them but to be bedridden for life, hooked to a pump?

Dr. Nose and his fellow researchers are working under a $1.2 billion government grant to perfect a miniature LVAD that can be installed permanently within a patient. They have set themselves a difficult goal, because not only would the implanted LVAD require the usual chambers and hoses, but a pump and electrical motor also—all inside the patient's body. No tubes or wires will run from the body to outside machinery. Power for the tiny electrical motor will come from an outside battery pack, which will transmit the electricity much the way a radio tower transmits electrical charges. As a further precaution, there will be an auxiliary power pack inside the patient's body, in case there is an interruption in the external power supply. A working model of this implanted LVAD is only about two years away.

Until the artificial heart is ready for use, LVADs—which might be referred to as partial hearts—will continue to help patients whose own organs either temporarily or permanently lack the ability to pump blood.

5. *The Pacemaker and the AID Defibrillator*
One of the best-known devices for helping out an ailing heart is the pacemaker. Most people have heard or read

about pacemakers and famous people—such as actor Henry Fonda—who continue to work at their profession with a pacemaker aiding the heart.

The healthy heart has a natural pacemaker. In the top of the right atrium is a group of muscle fibers called the sinoatrial (SA) node. The SA node generates an electric charge that travels through the atrial muscles, causing them to contract. This is known as the *excitation* wave. Separating the atria from the ventricles is a band of non-conducting fibrous tissue, which prevents the excitation wave from passing directly into the ventricles. Imbedded in the fibrous band is the atrioventricular (AV) node. This picks up the SA electrical charge and sends it through the fibers of the ventricle, creating a muscular contraction.

The weak link in this chain of electrical circuitry is the AV node. Anything that strikes at this portion of the heart endangers the ventricles, because they are then isolated from the initiating charge of the SA node. The heart can survive for years with no muscle function in the right or left atrium, but cannot live without the muscular contractions of the ventricles. Therefore, when there is a health problem near the AV node, a person needs an artificial pacemaker to keep the ventricular muscles contracting.

The first pacemaker was invented in the early 1950's. This model was worn externally, usually in a shirt pocket, and had wires leading from the device through the chest wall and into the heart. There were advantages to those first models because the wearer could adjust the heart beat to his needs. During the day, the heart could be allowed to beat a bit faster than at night when the wearer was sleeping. The disadvantage was the wires. No matter how careful the wearer was, infection inevitably traveled along those wires into the chest.

Therefore an implantable pacemaker was devised, which could be placed in the fatty tissue beneath the skin of the lower neck or upper abdomen. Later, pacemakers were sewn under the surface of the upper chest and neck region. The first under-the-skin pacemaker had a wire which was attached to the exterior of the heart. However, this wire would eventually work itself free and needed to be reattached, which could only be done surgically—reopening the chest cavity, which surgeons prefer to avoid. Modern pacemakers employ a wire—catheter electrode—that is threaded down the inside of a neck vein, through the right atrium and tricuspid valve and then comes in contact with a portion of the right ventricle. This wire, being held in place by both the vein and the heart, does not work itself away from the point of contact.

The power for the pacemaker's electrical charges comes from either lithium batteries or the more contemporary nuclear-power pack. The rate of pulsating electrical charges and subsequently heartbeats depends upon the type of pacemaker. The fixed pacemaker is set to send out electrical impulses continuously, keeping the heartbeat at a steady seventy-two pulsations per minute. However, not all heart patients need a continuous-assistance device, and for them the demand pacemaker measures the heartbeat, and when the rate begins to slow, it sends out electrical discharges to stimulate it back to a normal pulse. Once the heart is working well on its own, the pacemaker ceases its operation.

Recently, Medtronic, Inc. has offered a still more advanced pacemaker to heart victims. The new pacemaker, called Spectrax, is among the smallest (10 millimeters or about 3/8 of an inch thick) and lightest (45 grams or 1½ ounces) available today and can be tailored to meet an individual patient's pacing needs. The pacemaker can be programmed by the use of an external programmer. This allows a physician to change the pacemaker's function in response to a patient's changing medical condition at any

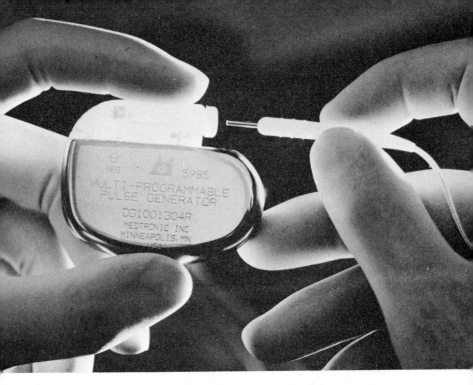

A modern, programmable pacemaker.

MEDTRONIC, INC.

The external computer by which it is possible to program the pacemaker.

MEDTRONIC, INC.

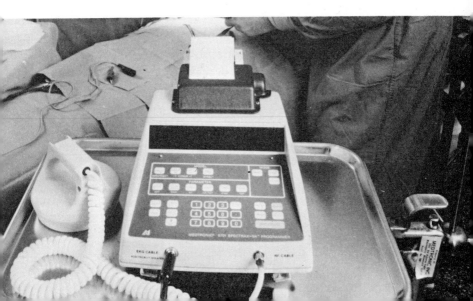

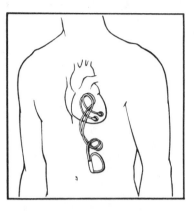

One type of pacemaker is inserted into the abdomen and attached to the outer muscle of the heart.

MEDTRONIC, INC.

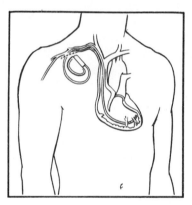

The more frequently used pacemaker is imbedded in the neck, and a wire enters the heart through a vein.

MEDTRONIC, INC.

time during his lifetime without subjecting him to another operation. The external programmer generates a burst of specialized radio-frequency energy that carries coded instructions, which tell the pacemaker to change the patient's heart rate, or the strength and length of the electrical stimulus.

Another company, Medrad/Intec Systems, has tested another heart assistance device—the AID defibrillator. The small, battery-powered instrument—about the size of

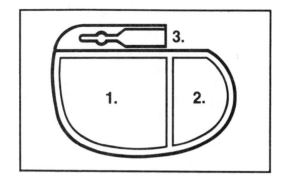

The three portions of a pacemaker: 1. The battery power source. *2. The* circuitry *where energy from the battery is transformed into a tiny electrical pulse. 3. The* connector *where the pacemaker is attached to the lead that enters the heart.*

MEDTRONIC, INC.

a small cigarette package—is placed under the skin of the upper abdomen and has wires leading to the heart. The AID defibrillator has been tested successfully in the prevention of cardiac arrest in patients who have a high risk of sudden death. The device will be especially useful to those heart patients whose abnormal heart rhythm cannot be controlled by drugs.

The titanium-encased device, weighing 9 ounces, monitors every heartbeat, recognizing potentially fatal heart rhythm abnormalities. Within 15 to 20 seconds of the detection of a problem, the AID defibrillator delivers the corrective defibrillatory jolts of electricity, and a possible heart attack has been prevented.

Actually, the AID defibrillator is a miniature version of the defibrillator machines used by ambulance crews and hospital emergency rooms to deliver electrical shock to abnormally behaving hearts—a potentially fatal condition called ventricular fibrillation, in which the heart beats at too high a rate. A pacemaker speeds up a too-slow heart, and a defibrillator slows down a too-fast heart. Also, the pacemaker works intermittently or continuously, while the defibrillator works only during a specific crisis. It was invented for the high-risk patient, to provide immediate correction *within* his body, because help from paramedical teams or rescue squads often arrives too late to save this kind of victim.

Although tested at Johns Hopkins and Sinai Hospitals in Baltimore, Maryland, the device is not yet on the market. However, company officials estimate the AID defibrillator will cost about $5,000.

THE ARTIFICIAL KIDNEY

New York Times headlines in the winter of 1980 once again focused world attention on the artificial kidney:

TITO'S DOCTORS SAY HE HAS PNEUMONIA
TITO, IN SERIOUS CONDITION, UNDER INTENSIVE TREATMENT
DIALYSIS MACHINE REPLACING KIDNEY FUNCTION FOR TITO

When people speak about artificial body parts, they usually mean devices which are inserted into the body. The artificial kidney, however, is not implanted. It is a machine which is connected to a vein in the person's arm and performs the kidney's cleansing function outside the body.

The story of the artificial kidney begins in the Netherlands just before World War II. At the University of Groningen, a young physician, Dr. Willem Johann Kolff, was placed in charge of a four-patient medical ward. One of the four, a twenty-two-year-old man, was dying from kidney failure, experiencing headaches, high blood pressure, and vomiting, and weakening every day. Dr. Kolff felt helpless. He realized that if he could remove a mere twenty grams of

Dr. William J. Kolff, the inventor of the artificial kidney, holds a model of his future dream—the artificial heart.

urea and other waste products from the man's bloodstream each day, he could relieve his suffering and possibly even save his life. The young man died. That experience launched Dr. Kolff on a single-minded campaign to find a treatment for kidney disease.

Kolff knew that if he could find a material that would filter the urea and waste products from the blood, he would

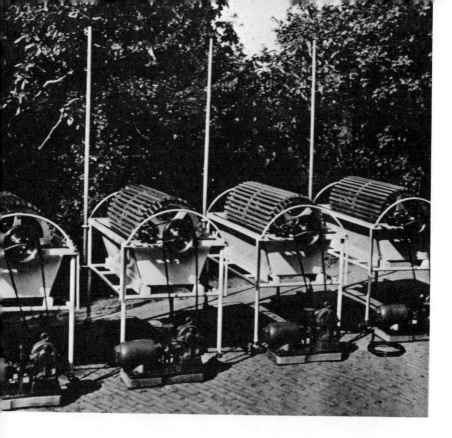

The first Rotating Artificial Kidney Machines, invented in 1944.

DIVISION OF ARTIFICIAL ORGANS—UNIVERSITY OF UTAH

have a method of cleansing the bloodstream. The principle on which he started work was the fact that molecules move through an area of high density to one of low density. For example, the air in a bicycle or automobile tire is pumped in under high pressure. Therefore, the molecules of air are tightly packed together—much more so than the air particles outside the tire. As a result, when the tire springs a leak, the molecules rush toward the area of less density outside the tire, and the tire deflates. It stops deflating when the density inside the tire equals the air pressure outside.

The same principal applies to blood passing through a tube submerged in a dialysate solution. The urea and waste products are more dense inside the tube than in the solution outside, so if the tube is made of a semipermeable substance—that is, material through which minute particles can pass, while coarser ones are held back—these water molecules would be drawn out of the blood into the dialysate. But finding the proper semipermeable material, which would permit only the undesirable products washing away, was the problem.

Kolff's experiments brought him to cellophane, which is a common substance today but was relatively new in the late 1930's. Filling a cellophane tube with blood, he immersed it in a saline solution for thirty minutes. The blood cells were too large to pass through the tubing, but urea, salt, and potassium, having smaller molecules, did move from the blood into the salt-water dialysate. Kolff immediately began on the next stage, which was producing a machine that would remove blood from a patient and cleanse, or "dialyse," it of impurities.

A patient attached to Dr. Kolff's first artificial kidney machine.

DIVISION OF ARTIFICIAL ORGANS—UNIVERSITY OF UTAH

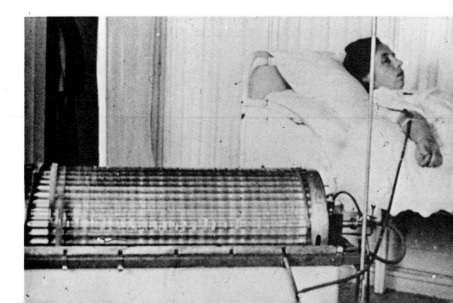

The German invasion of the Netherlands on May 10, 1940, brought upheaval into Kolff's life. A Nazi was appointed to head the medical department of the university, and Kolff resigned in protest, moving to a small hospital where he worked as head internist while continuing to refine his dialysis machine. But now he had another concern. The Nazis might steal his ideas, and he wished in no way to help them. During the next three years, keeping his research secret, he perfected the machine and discovered how to prevent blood from clotting while it was passing through the artificial kidney. Eventually he developed a device that rotated the dialysate as the patient's blood flowed through a cellophane tube.

In 1943, he began to test his machine. Of his fifteen experimental patients, only one survived. The others were in such poor condition that the new machine could not save them. Then, in September 1945, a sixty-seven-year-old woman was admitted to the hospital suffering from kidney disease. Although the patient was a known Nazi sympathizer, medical ethics demanded that Dr. Kolff do everything possible to save her life. He attached the dialysis machine and began cleansing her blood. The patient survived, and the Kolff Rotating Drum dialysis machine was a success.

Although this first dialysis machine was crude and clumsy, designed only for patients who needed temporary help for ailing kidneys, it was a landmark invention—the first machine ever devised to perform the function of a human organ. Medicine owes a large debt to Dr. Willem Kolff.

Modern dialysis machines, which are designed not just for temporary use but to enable the patient to be dialyzed indefinitely, nevertheless work on the same principle as Kolff's rotating drum. A tube of Silastic rubber is inserted surgically into the patient's arm or leg, forming a kind of

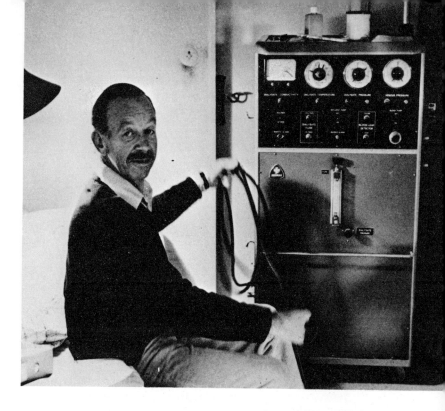

A modern dialysis machine.

shunt or bypass between an artery and a vein. As often as required the patient visits the dialysis unit of a local hospital, the Silastic tube is opened, and the blood floods out of the artery and into the dialysis machine. In the machine, a constantly circulating dialysate solution surrounds the cellophane tube, causing the waste matter in the blood to be drawn off. The cleansed blood is then returned to the patient's body by way of the Silastic tube and the vein.

New machines have monitoring devices to be sure that nothing can go wrong. An automatic switch-off is activated if blood begins diffusing into the dialysate or if air bubbles enter the blood. Still, the time required for the blood to be treated is the same as Willem Kolff used in his very first

A patient on an artificial kidney machine requires three tons of cleansing fluid, injections, clamps, tubes, water softeners and medication each year.

experiment with cellophane. The arterial blood leaves the patient, is cleansed, and reenters the vein a half hour later. Each dialysis treatment lasts from four to six hours, and most people need three treatments a week.

Although the artificial kidney has saved thousands of victims suffering from kidney failure, there are financial, emotional, and physical drawbacks.

Treatment at a dialysis center costs about $23,000 a year. Home dialysis machines are available, which reduce the expense to about $15,000 annually—including the machine rental and supplies. However, if the patient goes to the center, costs of dialysis are absorbed mostly by Medicare and the center itself, while those treated at home must pay at least 20 percent of the bills (Medicare pays the remaining 80 percent), and that comes close to $3,000 a year.

Psychological problems arise in many patients, too. First, three sessions a week, each four hours long, are time-consuming and exhausting. The patient cannot skip any appointment without endangering his life, and many kidney patients feel enslaved. Resentment toward the dialysis machine is sometimes so great that patients withdraw from treatment even though they know that death will probably result. Other patients develop a distorted image of themselves as unnatural creatures. Excreting urine is a normal function of everyday life, but dialysis patients never urinate. Others do not wait for slow death—emotionally disturbed, they rip out the Silastic shunt and cause themselves to bleed to death.

One remedy to these problems can be a kidney transplant, but, as shown, transplants are not always successful, and even many of those patients end up returning to dialysis machines.

Once again Dr. Willem Kolff has come to the aid of kidney patients. Today, he is working to develop the Wearable Artificial Kidney (WAK). The compact WAK weighs a mere eight pounds and is easily carried by the patient when strapped across the shoulders. The blood is withdrawn through one side of a Y-shaped needle, passes through the WAK, where activated carbon filtrates the wastes in the blood, and the blood then reenters the body through the other side of the Y-shaped needle. However, every fifteen minutes the WAK must be attached to an outside twenty-liter tank in order to remove the urea from the blood. Therefore, patients who use the WAK three hours a day, spend at least one and a half or two hours of that day attached to the tank.

An early model of the Wearable Artificial Kidney (WAK).

DIVISION OF ARTIFICIAL ORGANS—UNIVERSITY OF UTAH

The advantages of the WAK are great. The battery-powered device permits much mobility. People can work, walk about, vacuum the house, and even travel while their blood is being cleansed. Also, the general physical condition of a patient using a WAK is better, because the waste products are being filtered out on a daily basis rather than allowed to accumulate to a high level three times a week. When the machine goes on the market, the price will make it even more attractive: $2,500.

Another form of a portable artificial kidney has been developed by Dr. Jack Moncrief, codirector of transplant dialysis at Austin Diagnostic Clinic, and Dr. Robert Popovich, professor of biomedical engineering at the University of Texas. The colleagues have created the Continuous Ambulatory Peritoneal Dialysis (CAPD) technique.

The component parts of the CAPD seem remarkably simple when compared to the other artificial kidneys. A small tube is surgically implanted in a person's peritoneum,

Stephan Davis, a dialysis patient with a newer, more compact WAK.

DIVISION OF ARTIFICIAL ORGANS—UNIVERSITY OF UTAH

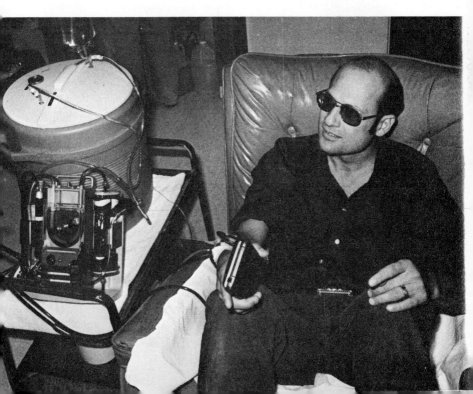

or stomach cavity. The patient takes a plastic bag containing two liters of dialysate fluid and hangs the bag up to let the liquid drain into the body through the peritoneal tube. When empty, the bag is rolled up and inserted into a small belt pouch. The patient.then goes about his business without any restriction because the additional two liters of body fluid present no physical problems. Four hours later, the bag is removed from the belt and set on the floor, and the fluid is allowed to drain from the body into the bag. That bag is discarded, and the patient empties another two liters into the body cavity. The process must be continued four times a day, seven days a week. The last "deposit" is made at bedtime and the first "withdrawal" of the day is made when the person wakes up eight hours later. If the patient maintains the CAPD ritual, he or she will never need to return to a dialysis machine.

The technique works much like other artificial kidneys. The peritoneum, the fine membrane surrounding the bowel, replaces the cellophane tubing of a dialysis machine. This membrane has an extremely rich blood supply. When the fluid is emptied into the stomach cavity, the waste products of the blood drain from the membrane into the dialysate.

CAPD has been so successful that dialysis centers throughout the United States and Canada have adopted the treatment method. At the present, 450 people have been liberated from dialysis machines and are now using CAPD to clease their bloodstreams. The cost is a bit more steep than WAK—between $8,000 and $10,000—but for most CAPD patients, complete mobility and the absence of embarrassing paraphernalia more than compensate for the financial investment.

From the first successful dialysis machine in 1945 to today's ultraeffective artificial kidneys into the future when additional portable kidneys will undoubtedly be invented, all kidney-failure patients alive today are there because of the man who first discovered the principle on which all artificial kidneys operate—Dr. Willem J. Kolff.

THE ARTIFICIAL LARYNX

Several years ago, Victor P. had the phone yanked out of his Schenectady, New York, apartment. The phone would ring, and all Victor could do was look at it or take it off the hook. Each sounding of the bell reminded the man, now sixty-eight, of something that he was unable to do and thought he would never do again: talk. Victor P. had not uttered a word since 1976 when his cancer-ridden voice box was removed in a laryngectomy. But now the phone is on its way back, and the next time it rings, Victor will be able to answer the call. A newly developed plastic tube and valve inserted through a surgically created hole at the front of Victor's neck has restored his ability to speak.

The plastic tube and valve assembly was introduced in 1979 by Dr. Mark I. Singer of the University of Indiana Medical Center and Dr. Eric D. Blom of the Indianapolis Veterans Administration Medical Center. Now the device has been licensed by the Food and Drug Administration (FDA) and is available everywhere in the county.

The surgical procedure is not technically complicated and takes only about 15 to 20 minutes to complete. Basically, it involves creating a small opening between the back of the trachea, or windpipe, and the esophagus, which runs parallel in the neck.

When the voice box, or larynx, is removed from the top part of the trachea in a cancer operation, the top of that biological "tube" is attached to the skin at the front of the neck. An opening, or stoma, is created that allows the patient to breathe. During the Singer-Blom procedure, a plastic tube is passed through the stoma, into the trachea and on through the surgical opening to the esophagus. The hole is kept open by the plastic tube until about 48 hours after the operation.

After being fitted, the device is ready to function. When the patient places a finger over the stoma, exhaled air from the lungs is channeled from the windpipe through a small hole in the plastic tube and into the esophagus. That air enables the patient to form words. The vibration of tissue and structures in the throat and upper esophagus create the sound. The Singer-Blom valve, which costs about $10, enables the patient to produce a normal-sounding voice.

The success of the treatment depends on the postoperative therapy. The patient must learn to relax, breathe with, and manipulate the device. Doctors are currently working on a valve for the tube's end at the stoma that would make it unnecessary for the patient to block the opening with a finger to speak.

THE ARTIFICIAL PANCREAS

The pancreas, a gland that is rarely longer than six inches and only a few inches in width, serves a most important function in the human body: it secretes digestive ferments which contain the hormone insulin. Widespread malfunction of the pancreas has resulted in the third highest cause of death in the United States—diabetes.

The pancreas is a racemose structure, which means that it is shaped vaguely like a cluster of grapes. The broad right end or *head* is nestled in the curve of the duodenum, while the rest trails off to a *tail* at the left of the body.

The pancreas has two purposes in our life-support system. First, certain pancreatic cells produce a clear, watery juice that contains enzymes. When released into the digestive tract, the pancreatic enzymes split fats, proteins, and carbohydrates into smaller molecules. Few problems arise with the gland's production of enzymes.

The second purpose of the pancreatic cells is to manufacture the hormone insulin, essential for the metabolism of carbohydrates, and to secrete that directly into the blood. This is the problem area. Naturally produced insulin is needed to maintain a normal level of blood sugar. As the amount of sugar in the blood builds, the pancreas releases insulin, which transports the sugar to the body cells, where it can be utilized as a source of energy.

But what happens when a pancreatic failure occurs?

Sugar builds in the blood and passes through the kidneys into the urine. Although there are other causes for diabetes—such an an inability of the tissue to use the insulin—the majority of cases are caused by a lack of naturally produced insulin. A victim experiences an increase in thirst and hunger, urinates frequently, and feels an itching sensation in the groin. There is marked fatigue, due to the loss of the carbohydrate energy. These symptoms are clues to a disease that can be fatal if not controlled. Although the most susceptible individual is the person who is forty or older and overweight, there is also *juvenile diabetes*, which strikes people under twenty. There are approximately 10 million diabetics in the United States today.

With the discovery of artificial insulin in 1922 by Dr. Frederick G. Banting and his assistant Charles H. Best, the usual treatment for diabetes consisted of having the patient inject insulin into his body or take insulin orally several times a day. Supplemented by strict diet control, this regimen enables diabetics to live quite normal lives.

However, a long period of using insulin—especially for those who develop juvenile diabetes—can produce problems. One difficulty is that insulin intake doesn't always maintain the proper amount of blood sugar. The fluctuation of levels occurs too quickly to time the use of insulin accurately. Even worse, long-term studies have proved that insulin-dependent diabetics have a higher risk of heart attack, stroke, kidney failure, and blindness than the average person.

Attempts have been made, at times successfully, to transplant a pancreas from a donor to a diabetic. One major block to an efficient transplantation program is that the pancreas "dies" within an hour or so of the donor's death. No effective process to preserve the organ for a longer period has yet been developed. And, of course, there is the ever-present problem of the rejection syndrome.

The solution is obvious—an artificial pancreas. Dr. Michael Ablisser, along with fellow scientists at the Biomedical Research Hospital for Sick Children in Toronto, Ontario, has designed one form of an artificial pancreas. The device weighs about a pound and is approximately the size of a pocket calculator. The diabetic carries the artificial pancreas alongside the body in a pouch. A tube, discreetly camouflaged, runs from the artificial pancreas into the patient's upper chest. Established dosages of insulin, based upon the user's height and weight, flow into the bloodstream, thus preventing too little or too much insulin being present at any one time. Further refinements are needed before this particular artificial pancreas is placed on the market. For example, Dr. Albisser and his associates believe the size can be reduced to that of a small ashtray. Also, the present pancreas, carried outside the body, restricts the user from any physical exertion that might dislodge the tube. The future pancreas will be surgically implanted inside the body near the collarbone. The wearer will then have more leeway in terms of daily activities, although he will still have to avoid strenuous physical actions. The "future" organ is only about five years away. Dr. Michael

Albisser expects to have the artificial pancreas on the market by 1986 or so, priced at approximately $2,000.

Meanwhile, Dr. William Chick of the Joslin Diabetes Foundation in Boston is working on another type of artificial pancreas. On October 22, 1979, *New York* magazine reported that Dr. Chick's pancreas is designed actually to replace the faulty body organ. The exterior is a man-made, semipermeable membrane shell, which will protect the artificial organ from tissue rejection. Lining this external covering are rat pancreatic cells. As the amount of glucose increases in the bloodstream, the rat cells respond by producing natural insulin, which passes through the membranous walls.

Long-term use of this natural insulin may eliminate some of the health problems previously discussed that occur when a person takes oral insulin or injections for many years. There is no projected date when Dr. Chick's artificial pancreas will be available to diabetes victims. The device has been tested with rats and larger animals, and the successful outcome has prompted Dr. William Chick to begin tests with humans.

Still another discovery was announced in July 1980. Researchers at Washington University Medical School, St. Louis, Missouri, have been conducting tests in which they injected mice with clusters of rat islet cells—the cells that produce insulin. When the cells were removed from the rats and placed in the mice immediately, the rejection syndrome arose, and the gland released chemicals that destroyed them. Therefore, scientists began to experiment with delayed transplantation. They removed the islet cells and grew them in a culture at room temperature for a week. Meanwhile, the mice were treated with a single injection of a chemical that temporarily suppressed their bodies' immune systems. Then the transplanted islets were injected into the blood, bypassing the pancreas with its destructive chemicals and allowed to collect in the liver, where they functioned without any apparent ill-effect on the mice.

Ten diabetic mice received these transplanted cells, which continued to function in the recipients' bodies. In seven out of ten mice, the cells produced insulin and maintained normal blood-sugar levels. The next step will be to attempt to transplant islet cells from pigs to mice, because that would mean crossing an even wider species barrier. This move is an important one, because if the method of treatment is to be used in humans, the source of the islet cells would be pigs.

However, these are only preliminary experiments. Scientists at WUMS estimate that application of these techniques to human diabetes is at least three to five years away.

In November, 1980, the world's first implanted insulin pump was placed in the body of a fifty-six-year-old diabetic man. A team of University of Minnesota—Minneapolis doctors, headed by Dr. Henry Buchwald, developed the artificial device which is the size of a hockey puck. The pump delivers a steady trickle of insulin into the bloodstream. Although Dr. Buchwald and his associates received permission from the Federal Food and Drug Administration to test the new invention, Dr. Buchwald wants everyone to be aware that this is the initial attempt to develop a perfect artificial pancreas.

"This is the first patient, and we're trying to acquire a lot of data," Dr. Buchwald stated in the November 8, 1980 *New York Times*. "This is after all an experimental procedure."

What perfections are needed?

One major drawback exists with the present model of the insulin pump according to Dr. Donald Bell, president of the American Diabetes Association. As of now the pump cannot vary the amount of insulin being released. There-fore, at meal times, when the blood sugar in the system rises, the perfect insulin pump should be able to increase the insulin supply.

Dr. Buchwald and his medical team are aware of this deficiency and will be working to add that refinement in a later version. Even without that capability, the present insulin pump, by keeping the insulin level more consistent that insulin shots or oral insulin, minimizes eye, kidney and blood-vessel damage that can afflict patients with severe diabetes.

As recently as sixty years ago, doctors could hope at best to keep their patients alive for two to ten years, depending upon the age at which the victim developed diabetes. Today, the means are almost within our grasp to counteract this chronic disease altogether.

PROSTHETIC LIMBS

The word "prosthesis", according to Webster's New Collegiate Dictionary, means, "an artificial device to replace a missing part of the body." Some people use the term to cover all the artificial body parts that are actually implanted. However, prosthesis is most often used to mean an artificial limb.

Artificial legs are easier to prepare and use than synthetic hands or arms, because they have less complicated functions to perform—supporting the wearer's body and enabling him to walk. The older artificial legs used straps to hold them in place, and certain models today still employ hardware to connect them to the body. But most contemporary prosthetic legs are attached by suction. A socket of polypropylene is placed over the leg stump. That will be covered by an inflexible outer shell. This exterior piece will be visible, and the socket is what grips the artificial leg.

Appearance is a vital consideration to the patient, so the artificial leg and the remaining natural leg must match. To achieve this, doctors use the surviving leg as a model. The leg is smeared with silicon oil, and a cotton "stocking" is pulled over the leg. Next, several coats of liquid silicone rubber are applied to the leg, and a stocking resembling pantyhose is drawn up over the leg. When the rubber has dried, the physician merely removes the mold like a sock. The silicone rubber mold is then turned inside out to make the opposite leg.

A rigid core is placed in the center of the stocking mold, and the remaining space is pumped full of polymer foam. When that hardens, the rubber stocking is taken off, and the artificial leg is completed. As a rule, patients need only a few weeks to become accustomed to using their artificial legs.

The processes of standing and walking are relatively simple operations. To stand, all we actually do is lock our knees in place. This is rather easy for the person wearing an artificial limb. A few weeks are generally needed before the patient walks without a limp, but there is a great psychological factor in favor of the patient. An almost desperate need exists to be mobile, to move again, so patients equipped with artificial legs will endure exhausting exercises and practice sessions just so they can once again walk.

There is another element to consider with artificial legs. And that's the cosmetic or self-image quality. For example, can a short person suddenly become a tall person? Men especially suffer from a loss of self-worth if they are short, feeling that tallness, for some reason, is more masculine. The answer according to doctors who work with patients suffering a limb loss is, no. Our limbs are in proportion to our body trunk. Tall people simply do not have longer legs—their body trunk is elongated in proportion to their legs, arms, and even neck. If a doctor were to prescribe legs

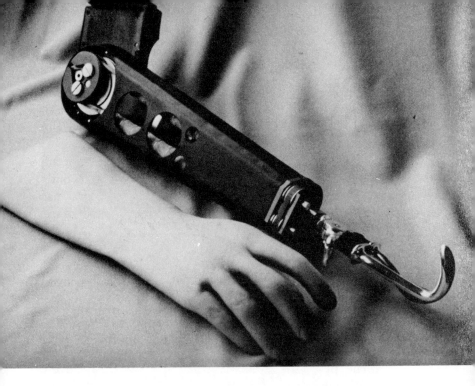

*An artificial arm: the mechanical gear and the plastic "cosmetic"
cover.*

DIVISION OF ARTIFICIAL ORGANS—UNIVERSITY OF UTAH

that do not match these basic proportions of the patient's
body, the person would have a "weird," disproportionate
appearance.

Although patients acquiring an artificial leg adapt
reasonably fast to that limb, artificial arms present other
problems. A majority of arm amputees never really develop
a facility with them. Straps and cables from the artificial
arm are wrapped around the chest and shoulders. To make
the arm move, the wearer must shift a shoulder by tugging
down or up. Other functions will only be completed if the
person tightens a muscle in the back or chest. The physical
movements needed to induce the motion in the artificial
arm can be physically tiring but also emotionally ener-

111

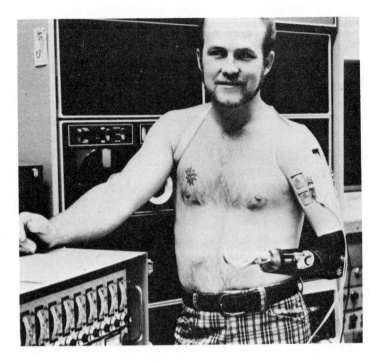

The "Utah Arm" designed by Dr. Jacobson and Associates. A computer is being programmed to tell the mechanical arm how to react to the patient's brain signals.

vating. When we shrug a shoulder emphatically and expect a major movement of the artificial arm, but see only a slight twitch, discouragement sets in fast.

Research has been going on, since the mid-1940's, to employ electromyographic (EMG) signals to operate the artificial arm. EMG impulses might be called muscular electricity. When a nerve impulse reaches a muscle, there is a slight change in shape of that muscle and the level of the electrical activity. A weak intention to move a joint produces a slight change in both, while a strong intention produces a definite change in shape and a sharp rise in EMG voltage. Scientists are trying to develop a means of taking the energy from other muscles in the body and sending it to the artificial arm. Unfortunately, no marketable product as yet has been produced for the wearers of artificial arms, although researchers at the University of Utah Medical Center are presently working on the prototype. If more easily produced flexibility can be induced into artificial limbs—especially arms—there will be greater rewards for the victims struggling to overcome their handicap.

In addition to loss of mobility, there is severe emotional damage to victims of amputation. Doctors have been able to help a majority of their patients adjust psychologically to the fact that they must wear an artificial limb by supplying cosmetically attractive, as well as useful, prostheses. With the experiments now underway, the time is near when they may be able to restore near-normal mobility to the new arm or leg.

ARTIFICIAL SKIN

Nearly 300,000 people each year are hospitalized for serious burns. As we have seen, those burns quickly become open wounds, highly susceptible to infection and permitting loss of heat, body fluids, and nutrients. In many cases, skin grafts from a patient's own body or from a human cadaver or even pigskin enable him to live long enough for the destroyed tissue to grow back naturally.

But what happens when there isn't enough skin remaining on the patient's body to supply grafts? Or when there is a violent immunological reaction against the donor's skin?

Previously, the answer was often death. Today, new solutions are being sought and found. Scientists at the

Shriner's Burn Institute in Boston and the Massachusetts Institute of Technology (MIT) have devised a semisynthetic skin to help burn victims.

The substance is composed of manufactured and animal material and can be used like a bandage of skin to shield burned areas of the body during the recovery period. The artificial skin has two plus factors, which at times make it more beneficial than real skin. First, there is no rejection syndrome present in any patient who has received the artificial skin. Secondly, the replacement pieces can be custom-made in a variety of sizes so that practically any burn—no matter how large or irregularly shaped—can be covered. This latest in artificial body parts was first used on selected patients in 1980. The results were positive, and MIT applied for a patent.

Still other tests on developing skin grafts for severe burn victims are being tested by Dr. Arthur Stein of the Albany Medical Center, New York. Under Stein's method, skin cells are removed from an aborted human fetus,* cleaned, and placed in a shallow culture dish filled with a nutrient liquid and lined with a thin silicone membrane. Within twenty-four to forty-eight hours of being placed in the culture dish, the cells grow into a thin layer on the silicone membrane. In about twelve days, the cells mature into a layer characteristic of normal skin and are ready to be placed on the burned area much like a bandage. Conclusive tests have yet to be conducted on Dr. Stein's method of growing skin, but it is an inspired concept in this important field of research.

The prognosis is that the use of artificial skin by medical facilities will soon be widespread throughout the United States.

---

*New York State guidelines for medical research require researchers to get the consent of parents and to confirm that the fetus is dead. In addition, Stein limits his work to fetuses which are less than ten weeks old.

Four

REPLANTS

With growing frequency, newspaper and TV news programs report on the newest branch of medical science: the replantation of severed body parts. For years, doctors have been able to restore a finger or toe that was cut off in an accident, but the replanted member retained little use. It is only recently, with technological advancements in microsurgery, that they can return the replanted body part almost to full usage.

Microsurgery is accomplished with tools much smaller and lighter than conventional operating equipment. Suturing needles, for example, are so tiny they cannot be held by the hand but are manipulated with specially designed holders. The tips of scissors are invisible to the naked eye. Surgeons have to wear special eyeglasses, similar to a jeweler's loupe, equipped with six-power lenses. Or they peer through a unique microscope, which permits two surgeons to view the operation through the same instrument. With these special tools, microsurgeons can perform operations of heretofore unknown delicacy. Ophthamologists use microsurgery to operate on the eye's retina. Ear doctors can restore hearing by reshaping portions of the middle ear. And surgeons have replaced the severed limbs of an accident victim.

Consider the wonders of several recent cases.

1. On May 20, 1980, fourteen-year-old William R. was making a pipe bomb in his Wantagh, Long Island, home. While he was filling a pipe with heads of safety matches, the device exploded. The blast ripped off his left ring finger and pinky. The volunteer firemen called to the scene immediately followed the most important rule when attempting to save a person's severed body part. They packed the two fingers in ice and rushed them with the boy to the nearest hospital. At the Nassau County Medical Center, doctors successfully reattached the two fingers. The surgeons feel that there will always be a slight stiffness in those fingers and a partial loss of agility, but at least the boy still has ten fingers.

2. On October 28, 1980, a twenty-eight-year-old man, whose name was withheld by hospital authorities, was working in a St. Louis, Missouri lumber company. While cutting wood with a circular saw, the man stumbled and fell onto the whirling blade, which severed his penis. The man's father, who was working alongside his son, helped him to an ambulance that rushed the victim to the Christian Hospital Northeast. During a five hour operation, Dr. Bela Denes, a urologist, and Dr. Wilfrido C. Feliciano, a plastic surgeon, reattached the severed organ.

"The early surgical result looked promising," Dr. Denes told an interviewer. "It appears viable."

Citing the speed with which the victim was rushed to the hospital's operating room—within an hour of the accident—as the main reason for success, Dr. Denes explained that he knew about only two other successful penis replants that have been conducted in the United States.

3. On March 31, 1977, nineteen-year-old David Jackson was working 1,000 feet underground in the shaft of a Kentucky zinc mine near his partner Jerry Duncan. Suddenly, overhead, a cable snapped, and a sheet of steel siding plummeted down the shaft.

"I heard that piece of metal fall," Jackson later said. "And Jerry was over in that shaft, the air vent, and I just reacted."

His reaction was to shove Duncan aside. Seconds later the sheet had sheared off Jackson's arms—the right arm just below the elbow and the left at the elbow. Jerry Duncan had his right arm severed at the shoulder and now wears an artificial limb.

What is Jackson's recollection of the moments immediately following the accident?

"Just for a second, I thought my arms were broken. They were numb." Also cut by the sheet was an air hose, and sand was blown in Jackson's eyes. "I finally got them open and saw what had happened. My arms weren't there."

Rescuers rushed him to nearby Carthage Hospital, where his arms were packed in ice, then on to Jewish Hospital in Louisville, Kentucky. Two teams of surgeons worked ten hours to replant David Jackson's arms. Since that time, Jackson has undergone five additional operations to return feeling and flexibility to his arms and hands. The most recent one, on March 14, 1980, grafted tendons into the left hand to improve his grip. Future surgery includes a bone graft into the left elbow and perhaps the installation of a plastic joint in that elbow.

Today, David Jackson can comb his hair and shave. He drives a car and goes fishing with his father. His fingers can tell the difference between hot and cold. Both as fun and for exercise, he even arm-wrestles his wife. He bears no self-guilt for sacrificing and nearly losing permanently his two arms for his friend's life. His actions prevented Jerry Duncan from losing his life instead of an arm. In fact, David Jackson said he would do the same thing again, even knowing the results. Duncan thanks Jackson for his life, and bears no bitterness that his own arm was too badly mangled to be restored, while Jackson thanks microsurgery for his two arms.

4. During 1979, the New York City subway system was plagued with a rash of senseless assaults—people shoved in front of oncoming trains. A thirty-nine-year-old man, Yong S. Sou, was killed when a mentally disturbed man pushed him onto the tracks, and a fourteen-year-old boy, fleeing a mugger, tumbled onto the track and was rescued mere seconds before the approaching train rumbled into the station. Perhaps the most horrifying incident was the one involving a seventeen-year-old classical flutist and soprano.

On June 7, 1979, Renee Katz of Flushing, New York, was standing on the subway platform at 50th Street and Eighth Avenue. Miss Katz, an honor high school student, had been accepted for a joint program at Tufts University and the New England Conservatory of Music. But at 8:14 A.M. on this June morning, she was headed for the High School of Music and Art in upper Manhattan to finish her final weeks of study before her June 21 graduation.

Suddenly an unknown young man rushed from the other waiting people and shoved Renee Katz onto the tracks just as a train was pulling into the station. The assailant then fled past the token booth, up the stairs, and into the street. Before the motorman could stop the train, the wheels of the first car passed over Renee's right wrist, severing the hand. After the train made an emergency stop, policemen and paramedics found the girl lying next to the cars. One officer immediately placed the hand in a plastic bag, while another ran to a nearby restaurant for ice in which to pack it. The victim was rushed to Bellevue Hospital. A six-person team of plastic surgeons, headed by Drs. Daniel C. Baker and William W. Shaw, then spent sixteen grueling hours restoring Renee Katz's right hand.

As soon as Renee was wheeled into the emergency room, doctors examined her to be sure she had no other life-threatening injuries. Miraculously, the girl had suffered no additional serious injury. They then began to give her intravenous feeding and rolled her into the operating room. A decision had not yet been made on whether or not to restore the hand (at times, a severed limb can be so badly mangled that even if it is reattached, it will never function), but in any case the open wound would have to be closed.

The six surgeons, two anethesiologists, and four nurses gathered in the operating room. The team was an experienced one. Only the week before, it had replanted a policeman's leg and performed similar surgery on a New Jersey chemical worker whose hand had been severed by a machine.

Dr. William W. Shaw, who had rushed from his office at the nearby New York University Medical Center, put on the special six-power eyeglasses called loupes. Cleansing the wrist, he put identification tags on the exposed tendons, nerves, veins, and arteries. Meanwhile Dr. Baker worked a few feet away, eyes pressed against a microscope eyepiece, removing dirt and debris from the severed hand. Prodding the blood vessels and other tissue, he was able to determine how badly they had been crushed. Then he labeled the exposed parts to match Dr. Shaw's tags on the wrist.

The moment for a decision had come. The microsurgical restoration of a limb is equivalent to doing seven operations at the same time. Was there a chance for success? First,

Renee Katz's age and general health were on her side. Also, her hand was crucial for her future career, so every possible attempt to restore the hand would be made. But what about the physical condition of the hand? Were the blood vessels, nerves, and tendons well enough preserved so they could be reattached? Yes. The operation would be performed.

Even as they began at 10:30 A.M., the surgeons knew this would be one of the longest of such operations on record. The first four hours were devoted to debridement, which means cleansing the wounds of tissue that was beyond saving and might hinder recovery, and freeing blood vessels and nerves that had been trapped and crushed by the injury.

We tend to think of surgeons as impersonal, slightly detached people, totally involved in their work. This team, accustomed to performing miraculous operations, is highly professional, of course, but the usual operating-room conversation was spotted with denunciations of the senseless crime and praise for the people who had helped Renee and had the presence of mind to pack the hand in ice.

Finally, at 2:30 P.M., the surgeons were ready to start connecting the hand. The bones had to be repaired first. If not, a broken piece of bone might later pierce a sutured vein or artery, destroying hours of work. Seven crushed carpal bones were removed from the site where the hand had been severed. An eight-inch metal rod was passed through an incision in the back of the hand and inserted into the radius, one of two bones in the forearm. Then Drs. Shaw and Baker, peering through their two-headed microscope, reattached the arteries and veins leading into the hand. Moments after the radial artery, which supplies blood to the back of the hand, was connected, Renee's hand turned a healthy pink. Two four-inch segments of a vein from Renee's foot had to be used during this important step.

At 9:30 P.M., the eleventh hour of the operation, the microsurgeons set about connecting the four flexor tendons in the palm and the four extensor tendons on top of the hand. By 11:30 P.M. the median and ulnar nerves were sutured. But problems arose.

There are two dangers to lengthy operations. First is the question of whether or not the patient can endure such long-term surgery. In this case, Renee's life signs were still strong. The problem was fatigue. Renee's surgeons were tired, but not so much that the weariness interfered with their skillful work.

At 12:30 A.M., the doctors worked on the palm of the hand. Another artery had to be repaired, which meant another hour of microsurgery. The thumb had been shorn of skin and the fingernail, so a skin graft from the thigh was executed. By 2:30, a new nurse shift had already arrived, and the operation ended. However, another two hours were needed to keep a constant check on Renee Katz in the recovery room, before the sixteen-hour ordeal was over.

What about the victim's future?

The surgeons can practically guarantee that the patient—after months of recovery—will regain some use of her hand. Another operation may be needed on the thumb. But the doctors doubt if Renee Katz will ever become a classical flutist. Virtuoso musicianship requires a dexterity that even the most successful replant cannot yet provide.

As for Renee's assailant, a man was later arrested for the crime, but conflicting testimony during the six-day trial caused the jury to acquit the man of the charges. No other suspect has been charged with the crime.

At 4:30 A.M., the doctors climbed into separate cabs and left for home—to meet again in the office at 7:00 A.M.

And so ended another "routine" day for the microsurgeons at Bellevue Hospital. These relatively unknown men and women go about their jobs each day and night, creating medical wonders as they replant severed body parts.

Five

THE FUTURE

Moral and Ethical Questions

Moving into the Age of Transplanted and Artificial Organs has created moral and ethical dilemmas for both patient and physician. Not only must the patient consult his private religious views, but doctors have been forced to reevaluate their own attitudes.

Religion is a personal thing for everyone. No religious group should be allowed to force another religious organization to accept its beliefs. So, each individual must form his own opinions. The Bible says there is a time to be born and a time to die. Does the transplanting of organs or implanting of artificial body parts offend this teaching by extending life beyond its alloted time? What about invasion of the sanctity of the body? And consider conflicting religious viewpoints?

On January 31, 1980, an Israeli student, Jesper Jehoshua Sloma, twenty-three, was shot in the head in the Israeli-occupied West Bank town of Hebron. A radical faction of the Palestine Liberation Organization (PLO) claimed to have done the shooting. The young man was flown to the Hadassah Medical Center at Ein Karem near Jerusalem. Unfortunately, the doctors could not save him. Slova's two kidneys were donated to Jerusalem's Shaare Zadek Hospital, where they were transplanted. One kidney patient was Jewish, but the second, Amira Abi Bukassah, was a twelve-year-old Palestinian girl from a refugee camp near the West Bank city of Nablus. The girl is claimed to have been outspoken about her support for the PLO and even wore a medallion bearing a PLO symbol.

Following the operation, ultra-Orthodox Israeli groups protested the kidney transplant. While Orthodox Jewish law prohibits desecration of the human body—in life or death—the furor centered on the fact that the kidney of a Jewish boy who had been murdered by Arabs was placed into the body of an Arab girl who had admitted her hatred of Jews, thus saving her life.

This incident brings up not only religious views, but political attitudes as well to be considered along with the medical concerns.

The effect on the medical profession has been even more severe. Physician members of an international group—the Transplantation Society—wisely saw the need to draw up the Code of Ethics.

The major battle facing them was arriving at a definition of death. Doctors were dogged with conflicting decisions. Which should be the principal concern, the life of the donor or that of the recipient? And should that decision be done on a personal basis? Take the case of an apparently dying donor and a rapidly failing recipient. Should the former's death be hastened to save the latter? One person might feel that the donor was so ill no recovery was possible and hence that the recipient should have his chance to continue living. Others might delay, hoping the donor would show improvement, leaving the recipient to approach the point where nothing would save him. Therefore, the Code of Ethics rules that brain death, rather than cardiac death, was the true definition. Sensibly, they built in a stipulation. This death had to be decided by two physicians whose primary responsibility was the care of the donor and who were independent of the transplantation team. By doing this, the society hoped to prevent a conflict of interest on the part of the doctors treating the recipient.

In connection with this, the society stated that transplanted organs from cadavers—when in acceptable condition—were preferable to organs from living donors. The reason for this is the medical belief that operations should not damage people, render them worse off than before. "I . . .will abstain from whatever is deleterious and mischievous," says the Hippocratic Oath. Consider a kidney transplant from a living donor. Almost every single living donor has been able to survive and live a normal life, but there have been a few deaths. Even one death is too many.

The society also decreed that no donor should be paid for the donated organ. This seems wise, but it solves no problems. There are still not enough of certain types of organs, and patients are dying because of this lack. Moreover, this decree tends to belittle blood transfusions and donations to sperm banks, putting them outside the realm of transplanted body parts, since those donors are often given financial compensation. In addition, ridiculous situations arise.

Mary Ellen Wolfe of Lakeside, Ohio, sixty-two years old, wanted to donate her body to science. The woman contacted the Medical College of Ohio in Toledo, indicating her interest. The reply she received was rather shocking—and not without a certain macabre humor:

> Though the donation of one's body to medical education is an act of selfless concern for the advancement of science, budgetary stringencies oblige the college to request a modest sixty dollars fee of each donor. Please enclose a check or money order with the completed forms, payable to the Department of Anatomy, Medical College of Ohio, in this amount.

In addition, the college officials wanted Mary Ellen Wolfe to pay shipping charges for transporting her corpse to the school. Understandably, Wolfe was furious and canceled the whole project.

Perhaps the knottiest problem concerned with transplants is the legal one. Who should decide when a donor may give an organ or when living relatives have a right to overrule the expressed desire of a dead man?

In England in spring 1980, during a flurry of heart transplants, a district coroner, Dr. Michael Charman, set himself in the surgeon's way. Under Britain's 1961 Human Tissues Act, a coroner's permission is needed as well as that of the relatives, when surgeons wish to transplant organs for which there is no written declaration from the dead person. The problem arose when a sixteen-year-old girl was killed in a traffic accident in Dr. Charman's district. Although the girl had signed a kidney-donor card, there was nothing in writing concening her other organs, but her parents nevertheless approved a transplant of their daughter's heart into another patient's body. Dr. Charman was infuriated when he was not consulted.

Should the parents rightfully be able to make the decision? Or should an outsider—in this instance a minor bureaucrat outspokenly against heart transplants—be allowed to obstruct such a case on a legal technicality? Since time is a vital factor in donations from the recently dead, should the law require officials to speed up the processing of sudden deaths?

A spokesman for the British Medical Association told the Associated Press, "People do die while waiting for a suitable heart. Anything that may delay the arrival of a new heart, even by hours, has an impact. If you are desperately ill, time matters."

The ultimate question deals simply with numbers and economics. Although no one wishes to view life purely in terms of dollars and cents, we must realize the end results of these marvelous advances in medical science are often astronomic and crippling expenses. Scientists speak about the "quality of life." But why replace organs with transplants or artificial parts, only to render the patient destitute or homeless because of his medical bills? Or destined to a life of loneliness? Or left to live as a mere vegetable? Have such people benefited from "medical miracles" or have they lost? Is a peaceful death preferable to a miserable life? And who should decide?

Also, much of the payment for operations comes from state or federal funds. If the number of such operations rises, should the public continue to provide financial support for heroic efforts to prolong life?

Lastly, even now, the world population is so great that many areas of the planet face starvation within fifty years. Prolonging life in people will eliminate the natural weeding-out process of death. Do we have the food supply and housing facilities to deal with an ever-increasing number of people? And should this world view even be a consideration when one is confronted with an individual case in which an organ transplant will save a life?

If the questions are complicated, the answers are even more elusive. Not only doctors, patients, medical societies and governmental agencies have to deal with these Gordian knots. Each person must eventually face his or her personal philosophy and conscience, to help determine the future routes that medical science should follow.

Donations Needed

A recurring theme in any discussion of transplanted organs is the heavy demand for donor body parts and the limited supply available. A barrage of news reports has alerted the public to this plight, but, ironically, although many people would like to donate organs after death, they find it difficult to initiate the process. Either they are not certain just how to go about handling the legal aspect, or they put off doing so. At ages twenty or thirty, few people are thinking about their death, so there always seems to be "more time to take care of that."

To encourage volunteerism, the National Conference of Commissioners on Uniform State Laws passed the Uniform Anatomical Gift Act, which has been approved by all fifty states. The bill allows any mentally competent person, eighteen years or older, to donate any or all of his cadaver to any hospital, accredited medical or dental school, university, organ-storage facility, physician or individual for use in scientific research, education, therapy, or transplantation. People who wish to donate organs need only stipulate such in their wills or by a signed, written statement with two witnesses. No one can overrule the signed document. Relatives are also permitted to allow organ donations, unless evidence is offered that the deceased would not have wanted it.

As beneficial as this new bill is, a problem often arises upon the person's death because these signed papers are locked in a desk somewhere. Perhaps those individuals who have made the legal provisions could wear a bracelet or necklace similar to those carried by people with specific health problems or medicine allergies.

Even with this law on the books, people are not making the necessary provisions. Some states have helped by providing the means by which they can register, but problems occur. For example, New York State passed a law stating that each person's driver's license would contain a section where the licensee could sign, indicating that he agreed to donate one or more organs.

However, the Motor Vehicle Bureau (MVB) maintains that the licenses are already packed so full of information that there is no room to add still more. Consequently, they had separate cards printed up, which applicants could obtain at MVB offices. The trouble with this system is that few people know about the cards or bother to obtain them, and when they do, the card is kept separate from the license. When an accident occurs, the signed card may be located too late for organs to survive for donation. In 1981, when New York driver's licenses will require photographs, officials of the MVB hope to add the donor statement to the license itself.

Some organizations have printed donor cards and will provide those to anyone requesting them. For example, the National Kidney Foundation, 2 Park Avenue, New York, New York, 10016, will send a universal-donor card to anyone who requests the paper.

What happens when you offer to donate an organ to an organization like the National Kidney Foundation?

Many people may be surprised to learn that potential donors are given psychological tests to determine if they are truly "sound in mind" when they offer to volunteer body parts. Organizations also want to be sure that the person is not being coerced in some way and is not working on the assumption that financial payment will be made for the donated organ. Following the psychological testing, the prospective donor is given a medical checkup and a vigorous search is made into his health history to ascertain that

A universal-donor card.

NATIONAL KIDNEY FOUNDATION, INC.

there are no physiological reasons why certain organs
should not be accepted. Hereditary traits are explored at
this same time to learn that no genetic defects are present
in the donor.

Meanwhile, physicians will be conducting matching
tests to determine if the organ matches the recipient's
immunological system. In the early 1970's, the National
Transplant Communications Network was founded in Los
Angeles, California. The group specializes in kidneys only,
but people in the United States and Canada who wish to
donate a kidney are invited to register. The Network provides a service for doctors. For example, a physician in Los
Alamos, New Mexico, who has a patient needing a kidney
transplant can learn that there is a matching donor in
Augusta, Maine. Transporting the organ is easier than
moving the patient, so the kidney is flown to the city where

a kidney-failure patient is awaiting the transplant. A similar organization, Eurotransplant, operates throughout Western Europe.

But the pounding, vital message is that *donors are desperately needed.* For instance, the average waiting time for a kidney transplant is fifteen months, and some patients have waited up to seven years for a matching kidney. These individuals are on weekly dialysis treatments and also a waiting list at the hospital. Organs are also needed for research. Frequently a donated organ is sent to a recipient because the body part can mean the difference between life and death. Yet research institutes also need organs to conduct experiments designed to perfect transplant operations. We can't allow someone to die if it can be prevented, so the patient has first priority, but today's lack of organs may mean that people will die tomorrow because a needed technique has not been perfected.

How are willing donors to be reached? And *reached* may indeed be the key word. Organizations need to develop a means of making contact with the people themselves—not through mail or newspaper articles. Think of the blood drives in communities, where medical people bring their facilities right to large factories or corporations so that the average person needs only to walk into the company's clinic or the parking lot where a trailer is staffed and equipped to receive a blood donation. Perhaps another answer of "touching" people may lie in the telethon method which has done so much for other health organizations. Entertainers and victims truly "touch" the viewers' hearts, and the television watcher responds by sending in donations. Admittedly, it is easier to send a few dollars than to give a portion of your body—even in the future—but more people might well sign donor cards if they merely have to dial a telephone number to begin the process.

Whatever the answer, until a more plentiful supply of

donated organs of all types is available, patients will continue to weaken and die. As sad as death may be, the real tragedy is that there *are* people who would be willing to donate organs, but the supply has not been successfully tapped.

Tomorrow

What is the future for transplanted and artificial organs? Limitless.

Obviously, certain major problems must still be overcome. The rejection syndrome continues to plague transplant patients as well as the limited supply of needed body parts. Other needs are not yet satisfied. For example, certain infants are highly allergic to milk formulas sold in the stores and must have breast milk to survive. In February 1980, Governor Hugh Carey of New York State suggested in his State-of-the-Health message that breast-milk banks be organized and that the state should "promote the breast-feeding of all infants" to prevent diseases "associated with the ingestion of artificial foods."

Even larger, seemingly unattainable goals lie ahead: the artificial heart and the artificial brain. At the moment, even contemplating an artificial brain seems eons away, but this field of medical technology is perhaps the fastest moving of all scientific areas. Weekly, news reports of substantial discoveries appear in newspapers, magazines, or on television, one following on the heels of the other.

If Juan Ponce de Leon sought the Fountain of Youth along the coast of Florida, we can realistically search for it in the laboratories and operating rooms of today's medical and research centers. And if Ponce was viewed as a fool in his quest, today's medical scientists are seen as miracle workers.

BIBLIOGRAPHY

Books

Balner, Hans, *Bone Marrow Transplantation and Other Treatment After Radiation Injury.* Boston: Kluwever Boston, Inc., 1977.

Barnard, Christiaan N., *One Life.* New York: Macmillan, 1969.

Blaiberg, Philip, *Looking at My Heart.* New York: Stein and Day, 1968.

Cowan, Kenneth, *Implant and Transplant Surgery.* Levittown, New York: Transatlantic Arts, Inc., 1972.

Deaton, John G., M.D. *New Parts For Old.* Palisade, New Jersey: Franklin Publishing Company, Inc., 1974.

Fishlock, David, *Man Modified.* New York: Funk and Wagnalls, 1969.

Freese, Arthur S., *The Bionic People Are Here*. New York: McGraw-Hill Company, Inc., 1979.

Gerrick, David J., *Transplants in Man*. Dayton, Ohio: Dayton Labs, Inc., 1978.

Longmore, Donald, *Spare-Part Surgery*. New York: Doubleday & Company, Inc., 1968.

Miller, George W., *Moral and Ethical Implications of Human Organ Transplants*. Springfield, Illinois: Charles C. Thomas, Publisher., 1971.

Nizsalovskzky, Endre, *Legal Approach to Organ Transplantation*. New York: International Publications Service, Inc., 1975.

Nolan, William A., *Spare Parts for the Human Body*. New York: Random House, Inc., 1971.

Serafin, Donald and Harry Buncke. *Microsurgical Composite Tissue Transplantation*. St. Louis: C.V. Mosby Company, Inc., 1978.

Skurzynski, Gloria, *Bionic Parts For People*. New York: Four Winds Press, 1978.

Thorwald, Jürgen, *The Triumph of Surgery*. New York: Pantheon Books, 1960.

Warshofsky, Fred, *The Rebuilt Man*. New York: Thomas Y. Crowell Company, 1965.

Periodicals:

"The Ambiguity of Organ Transplants," *The Christian Century*, April 2, 1980.

"Artificial Organs and Beyond," *Science News*, September 3, 1977.

"Artificial Organs: Replacing the Irreplaceable," *New York*, October 22, 1979.

"Diabetic Rats Cured by Islet Transplant," *Science News*, April 21, 1979.

"From Death to Life," *Good Housekeeping*, February, 1980.

"Insulin Pump for Diabetics," *Newsweek*, March 26, 1979.

"It Won't Hurt, 'cause You're My Brother," *Reader's Digest*, March, 1979.

"Microsurgery," *Newsweek*, June 25, 1979.

"New Hips for Old," *Modern Maturity*, February-March, 1972.

"New Hope for Burn Victims," *Reader's Digest*, June, 1979.

"New Parts for Your Body," *Family Health*, March, 1980.

"One Answer to Childlessness—Artificial Insemination," *Science Digest*, March, 1980.

"One Week With an Artificial Heart," *Hospital Physician*, November, 1971.

"Organ Transplants: What We Now Know," *McCalls*, February, 1979.

"Overcoming Transplant Rejections," *Harper's Bazaar*, September, 1977.

"The Replacement-Parts Dilemma: Who Should Give, Who Receive?" *Science Digest*, November, 1979.

"Professor Charnley's Marvelous Hip," *Reader's Digest*, August, 1975.

"Second Skin," *Newsweek*, February 2, 1976.

"Souls on Ice," *Esquire*, April, 1980.

"Superkids?" *Time*, March 10, 1980.

"Surgical Replacement of the Human Knee Joint: Pherocentric Prosthesis," *Scientific American*, January, 1978.

"Testicle Transplant: Case of Twins Terry and Timothy Twomey," *Newsweek*, June 6, 1977.

"Transplants and Compassion," *The Christian Century*, March 5, 1980.

"Transplant Technology Today: A Scoreboard + the Outlook," *Science Digest*, December, 1979.

Newspapers:

"Antigens May Prove Key to Organ Transplantation," *New York Times*, October 11, 1980.

"Artificial Skin Developed at MIT," *The Recorder* (Amsterdam, New York), July 12, 1980.

"Behind Renee Katz Case: Tangled, Scant Evidence," *New York Times*, February 19, 1980.

"Bone Marrow Transplants Saving More and More Lives," *The Recorder* (Amsterdam, New York), September 19, 1980.

"Boy's Fingers Lost in Blast Restored," *New York Times*, May 22, 1980.

"British Transplants Ruling Raises Furor," *Schenectady* (New York) *Gazette*, March 11, 1980.

"Briton's Condition is Called Good After Heart Transplant Operation," *New York Times*, February 24, 1980.

"Burn Center Sets up First Skin Bank in New York," *New York Times*, April 2, 1978.

"Carey Proposes State Mother's Milk Banks," *Schenectady* (New York) *Gazette*, February 28, 1980.

"Dialysis Machine Replacing Kidney Function for Tito," *New York Times*, February 23, 1980.

"Doctors Restore Student's Hand, Severed by Train," *New York Times*, June 9, 1979.

"Doctors Say Device Aids Heart Patients," *New York Times*, August 7, 1980.

"Fetal Skin Grafts for Burns Studied," *Schenectady* (New York) *Gazette*, November 7, 1979.

" 'Hearing Dogs' Being Developed as a Service to Deaf Persons," *The Recorder* (Amsterdam, New York), October 24, 1980.

"High Fever is Threatening Tito," *New York Times*, March 15, 1980.

"How Delicate Surgery Saved a Hand," *New York Times*, June 12, 1979.

"Insulin-Pump Implant is a First," *New York Times*, November 8, 1980.

"Medical Team Transports Liver Across the Country in Cooler," *Schenectady* (New York) *Gazette*, May 13, 1980.

"Mother's Milk Sought to Aid Columbia County Toddler," *Knickerbocker News* (Albany, New York), November 23, 1979.

"New Frontiers in Conception," *New York Times*, July 20, 1980.

"Ohio Woman Furious over 'Stiff' Charges," *Schenectady* (New York) *Gazette*, January 23, 1980.

"Penis Cut Off by Buzz Saw Sewn Back," *New York Post*, November 3, 1980.

"Plastic Tube Offers Solution to Terrible Problem," *Schenectady* (New York) *Gazette*, August 26, 1980.

"Replacement Surgery Brings Light to Cataract Victims," *Schenectady* (New York) *Gazette*, June 23, 1980.

"Scientists Transplant Insulin-Growth Cells," *Schenectady* (New York) *Gazette*, July 9, 1980.

"The Search for a 'Bionic' Heart," *New York Times*, October 21, 1979.

"Second Skin Graft for Pryor 'Successful'," *Schenectady* (New York) *Gazette*, July 3, 1980.

"Severed Arms Restored, Miner Glad He's Able to Shave," *Schenectady* (New York) *Gazette*, April 21, 1980.

"Sex Transplant Man a Dad," *Schenectady* (New York) *Gazette*, March 27, 1980.

"Shortage of Kidneys for Transplant Lingers On," *The Recorder* (Amsterdam, New York), February 9, 1980.

"Single Woman Refused Option of Artificial Insemination," *The Recorder* (Amsterdam, New York), July 16, 1980.

"Three Cell Researchers Win Medicine Nobel," *New York Times*, October 11, 1980.

"Three of Four Severed Fingers are Reattached," *Schenectady (New York) Gazette*, October 23, 1980.

"Tito's Doctors Say He Has Pneumonia," *New York Times*, February 24, 1980.

"Tito, in Serious Condition, Under Intensive Treatment," *New York Times*, February 25, 1980.

"Transfusions Help Kidney Transplants," *Schenectady* (New York) *Gazette*, April 26, 1980.

"A U.S.-Backed Show: From the Bifocal Lens to the Artificial Heart," *New York Times*, May 25, 1980.

INDEX

Index